ABOUT THE GUITARIST'S SCALE BOOK

The *Guitarist's Scale Book* is the most accessible, most complete scale reference you will find. It is accessible because the scales are arranged alphabetically (so you don't need to be a master of music theory to find what you're looking for), and with our *Scalefinder System*, the scale you seek is literally at your fingertips.

It is complete because it includes major, minor, and pentatonic scales in every key, along with almost every other scale and mode imaginable. It includes suggestions on how to use each scale. It includes explanations of scale and mode theory, concise explanations that even a beginner can understand. It includes cross-stringing scales and even a special section featuring exotic, foreign scales.

Used alone, *The Guitarist's Scale Book* is an indispensable reference for every guitar player. Used in conjunction with *The Guitarist's Chord Book* and the *Let's Jam!* CDs, *The Guitarist's Scale Book* becomes part of a complete learning package for the teacher or student.

WHO THIS BOOK IS FOR

The Guitarist's Scale Book was written by a professional, but designed with the knowledge that you may not be a professional. Perhaps you're a beginner in need of a quick, simple way to find the scales you don't know. Perhaps you've been playing for years and want to add new scales to your repertoire. Or maybe you're a teacher in search of the ideal scale reference for your students. If you fall into any of these categories, then *The Guitarist's Scale Book* is for you.

ABOUT THE AUTHOR

Peter Vogl has earned his living by playing and teaching guitar since he was 25. He wrote his first instruction book 15 years ago and thousands of people have learned to play the guitar using his manuals and videos. Peter has personally taught a great number of students, both individually and in university classrooms. Most importantly, Peter still teaches today.

Though he plays and records professionally, Peter hasn't lost touch with what a beginner knows and doesn't know. He understands the best way to present material for both the student and the teacher. He has put that understanding and his years of professional experience to work in *The Guitarist's Scale Book*.

TABLE OF CONTENTS

HOW TO USE THE SCALE BOOK

Our **Scalefinder System** helps you quickly find each scale. Close the book and put your thumb and index finger over the icon on the cover. You'll see a black line. Flip to that page and the scales will be at your fingertips.

M A J O R

Left Hand Fingering

1 = index finger
2 = middle finger
3 = ring finger
4 = little finger

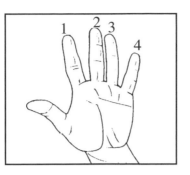

At the top of many pages you will find information about the scales. The scale degrees are always in comparison to a major scale. For example, if the scale degree is a flat 3, that means it is flatted in relation to a major scale. The interval is the distance between the notes in the scale (half step equals one fret, whole step equals two frets). There is also music notation to show the scale in the treble clef.

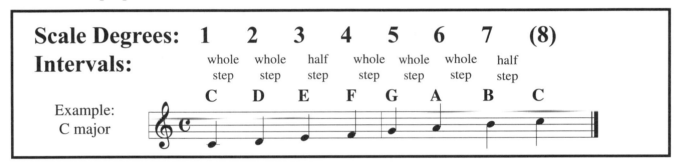

In the middle of the page you will find scale diagrams showing multiple patterns for each scale. Pay attention to the grey circles. They represent the *tonic* or *root* (the note that names the scale). For example:

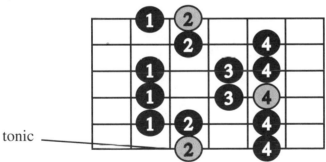

At the bottom of many pages you will find descriptions of the scale, suggestions for usage, and notes on theory. Read these sections to get ideas on how to use these scales. For example:

The major scale is a seven-note scale. All of the other scales will use the major and minor scales for comparison.
Suggestions for usage: Primarily used over major chords and tunes in a major keys. May be used over any type of music.
Example: C major scale over CM7. Try E major over track 11 and Bb major over track 13 of the *Let's Jam! CD Blues & Jazz.*

READING TABLATURE

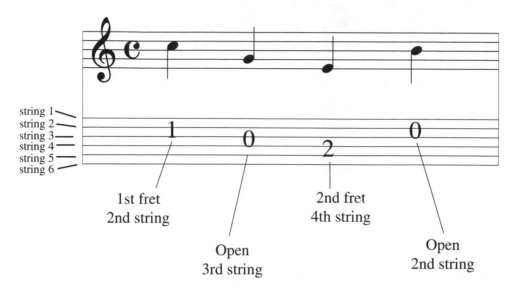

string 1
string 2
string 3
string 4
string 5
string 6

1st fret
2nd string

Open
3rd string

2nd fret
4th string

Open
2nd string

The six lines below the treble clef are called *tablature*. Each line represents a string of the guitar. The lowest line represents string number six. The highest line represents string number one. The number on the string represents the fret to be played. A number "1" indicates the first fret. The "0" means play an open string.

SCALE DIAGRAMS

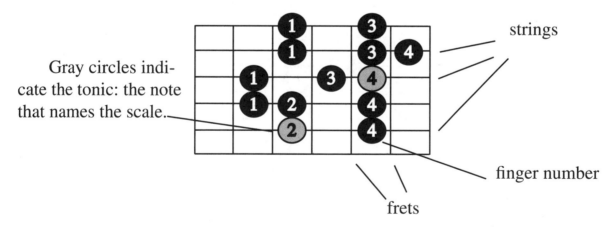

Gray circles indicate the tonic: the note that names the scale.

strings

finger number

frets

FULL NECK DIAGRAMS

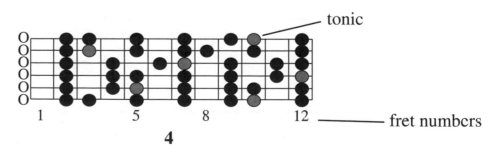

tonic

1   5   8   12 ——————— fret numbers

4

THE GUITAR NECK

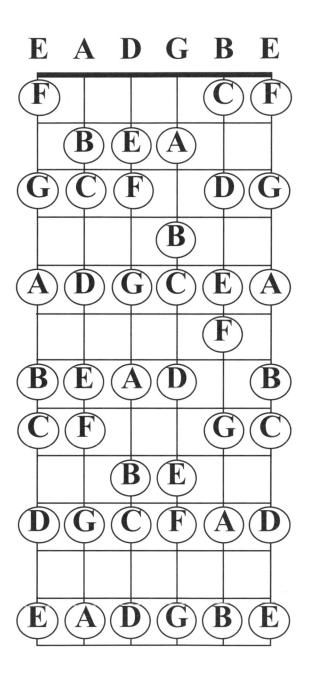

THE MAJOR DIATONIC SCALES

Scale Degrees:	1	2	3	4	5	6	7	(8)
Intervals:		whole step	whole step	half step	whole step	whole step	whole step	half step

Example: C major — C D E F G A B C

MAJOR SCALE PATTERNS

The gray circles represent the tonic (the note that names the scale).

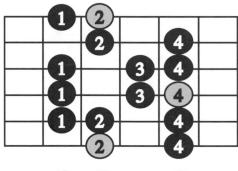
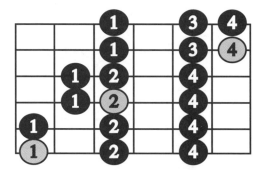
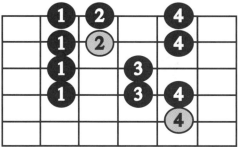
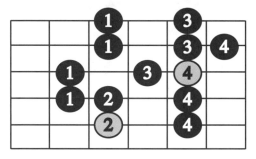
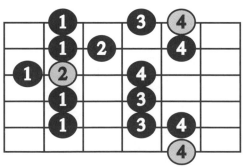

The major scale is a seven-note scale. All of the other scales will use the major and minor scales for comparison.

Suggestions for usage: Primarily used over major chords and tunes in a major keys. May be used over any type of music.

Example: C major scale over CM7. Try E major over track 11 and Bb major over track 13 of the *Let's Jam! CD Jazz & Blues.*

A MAJOR

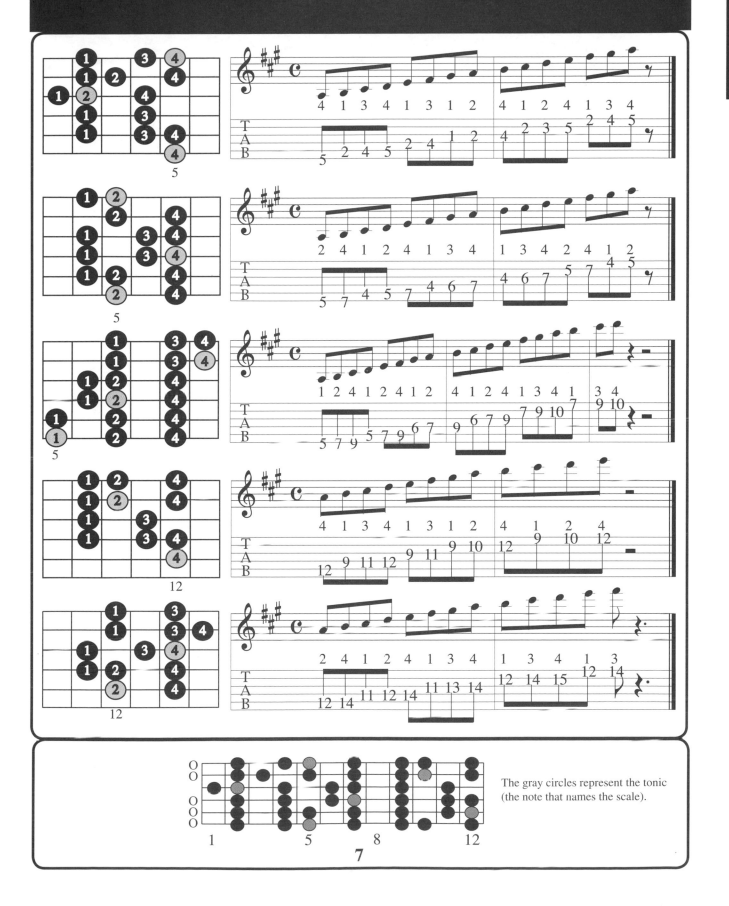

The gray circles represent the tonic (the note that names the scale).

7

Bb MAJOR

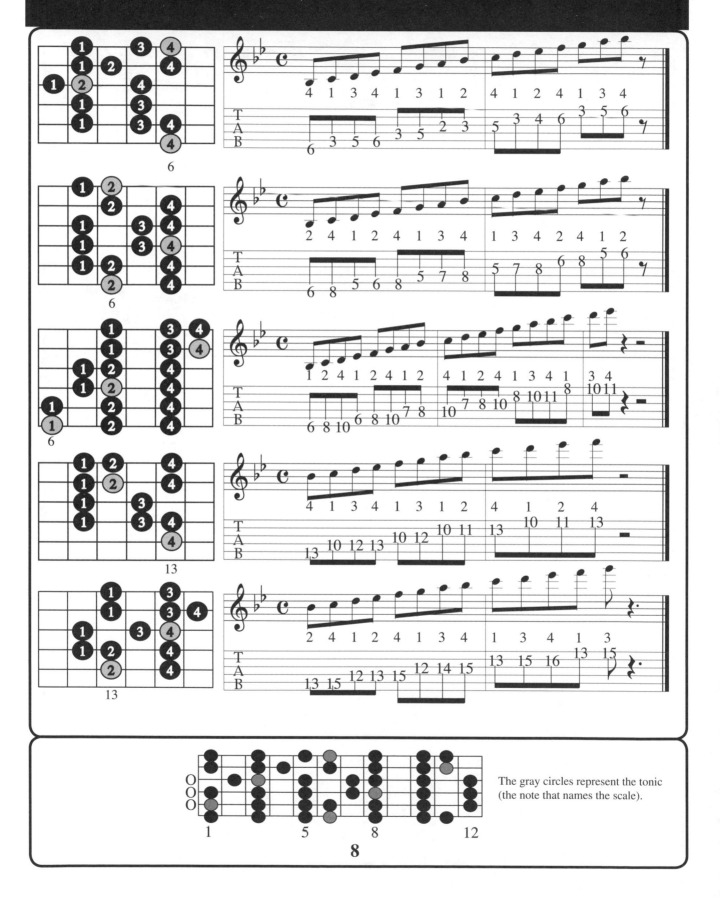

The gray circles represent the tonic
(the note that names the scale).

B MAJOR

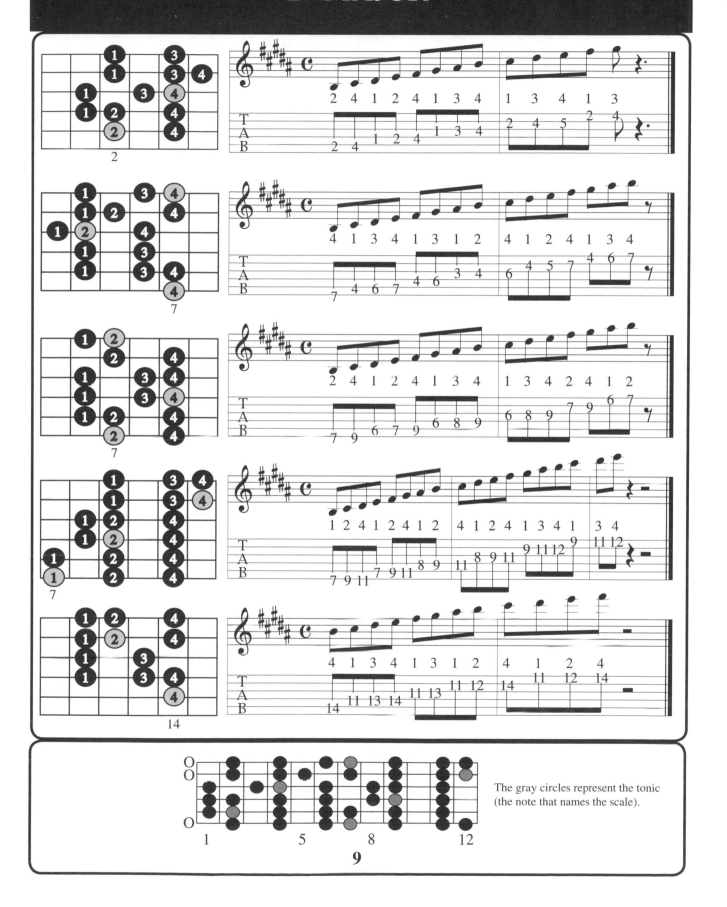

The gray circles represent the tonic (the note that names the scale).

C MAJOR

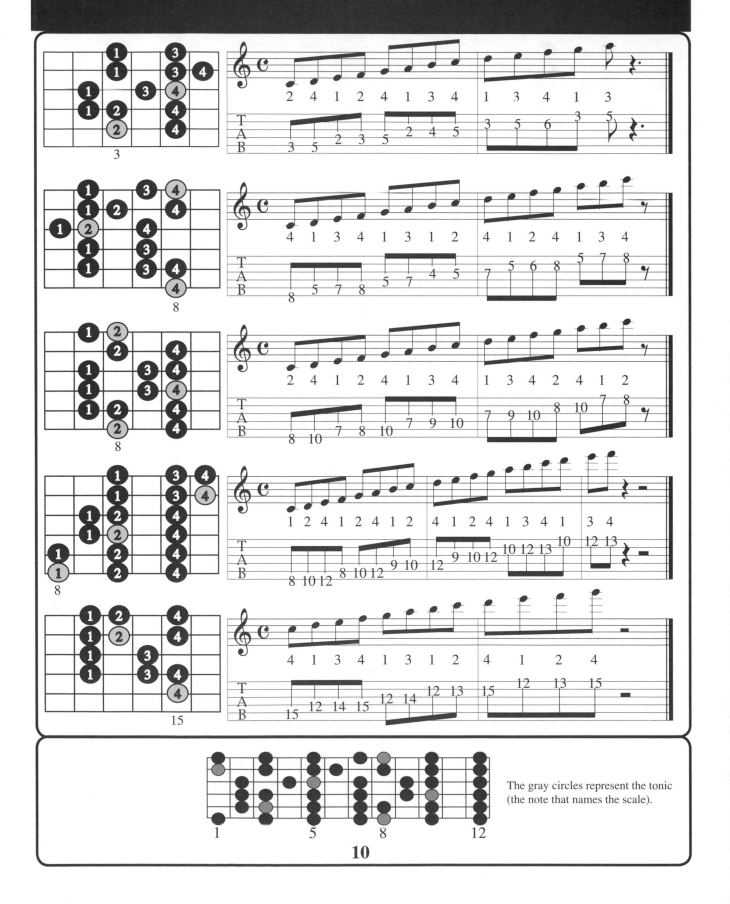

The gray circles represent the tonic (the note that names the scale).

10

C# MAJOR

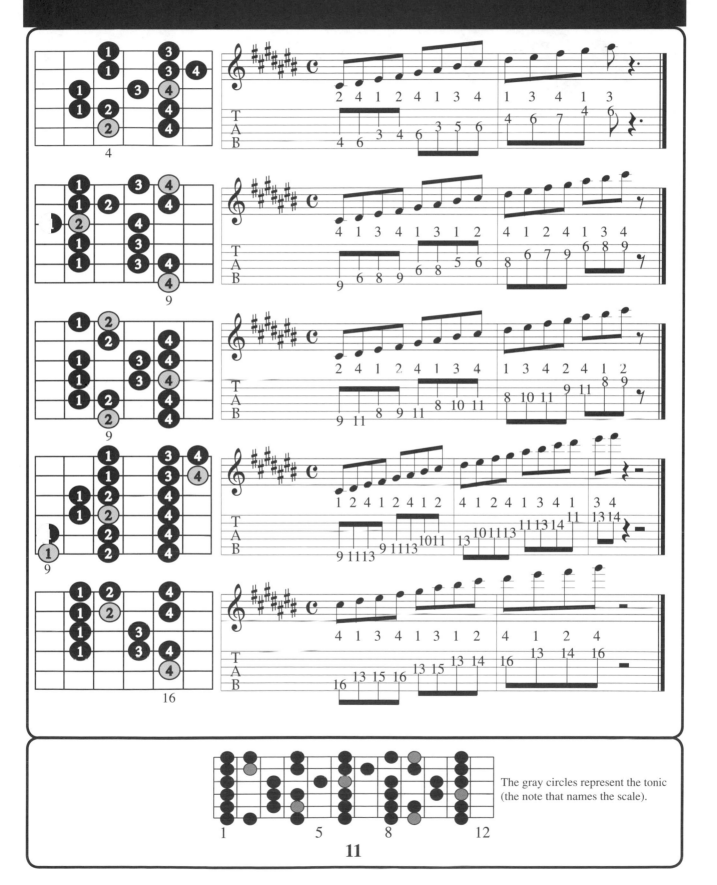

The gray circles represent the tonic (the note that names the scale).

11

D MAJOR

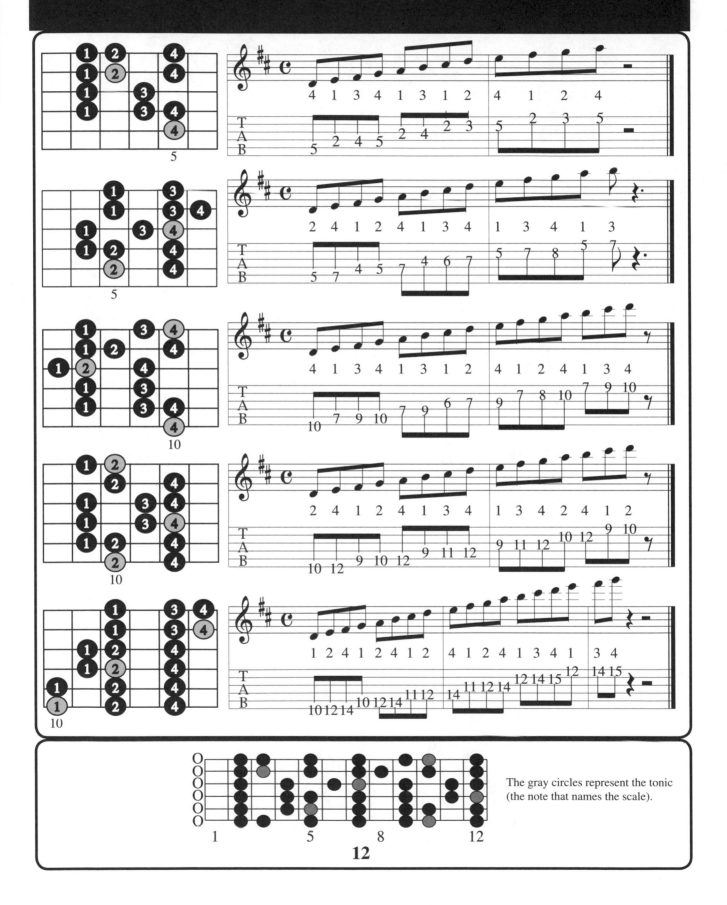

The gray circles represent the tonic (the note that names the scale).

Eb MAJOR

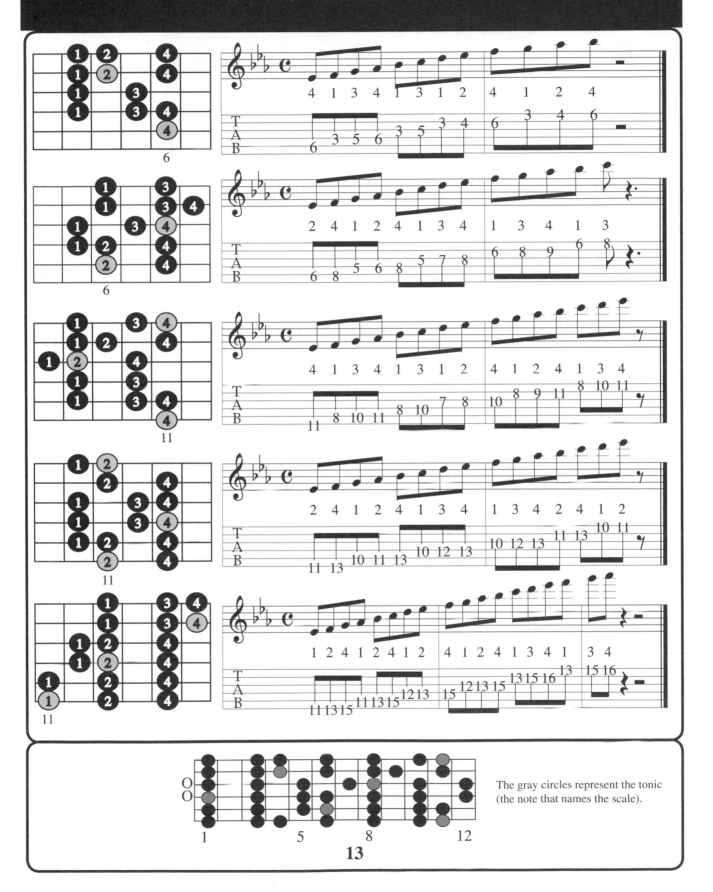

The gray circles represent the tonic
(the note that names the scale).

13

E MAJOR

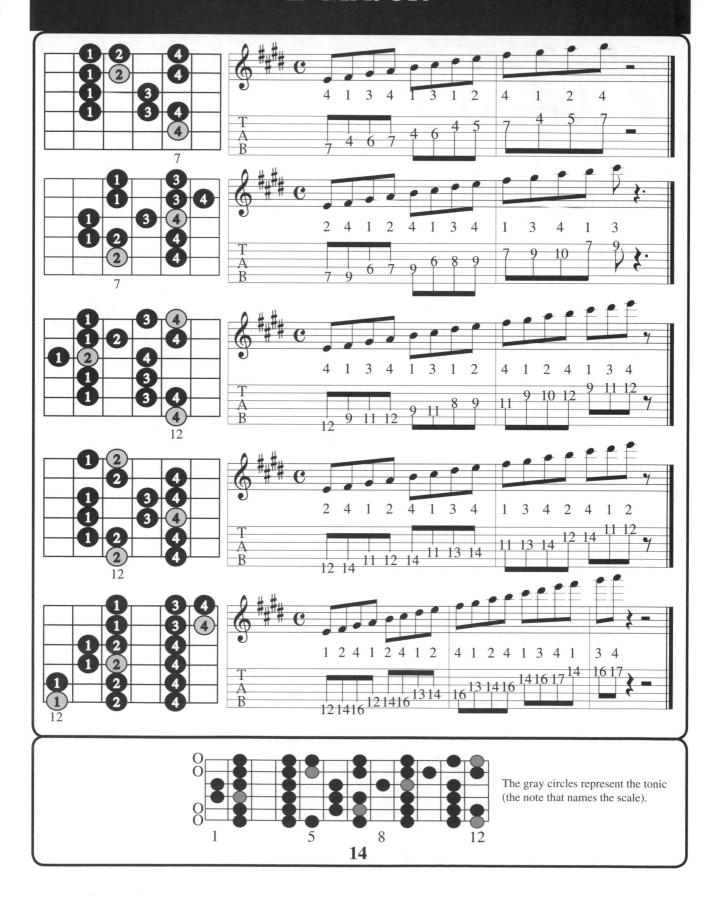

The gray circles represent the tonic (the note that names the scale).

F MAJOR

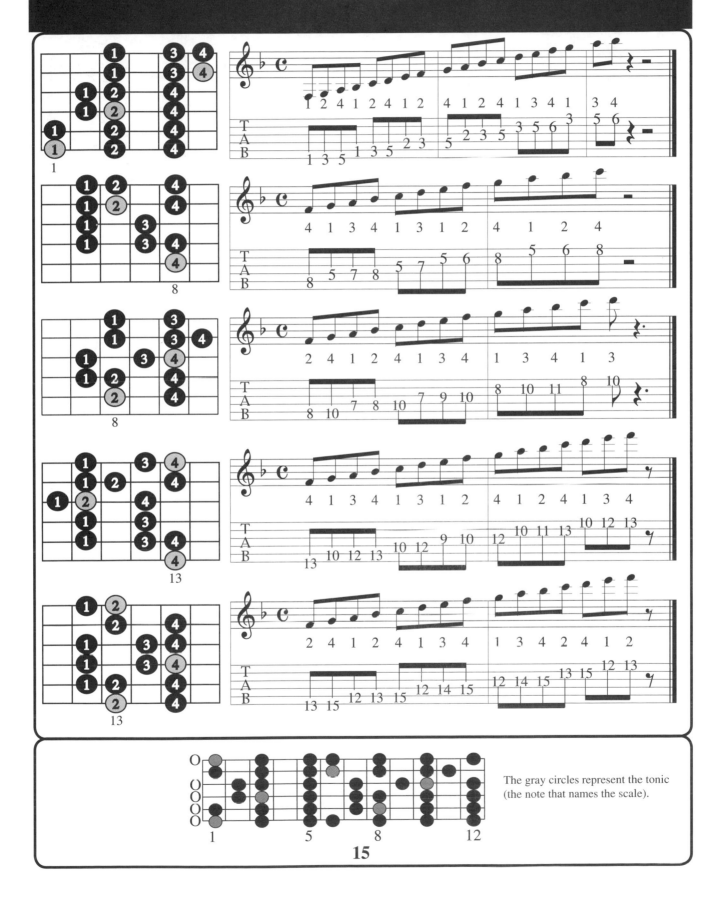

The gray circles represent the tonic (the note that names the scale).

15

F# MAJOR

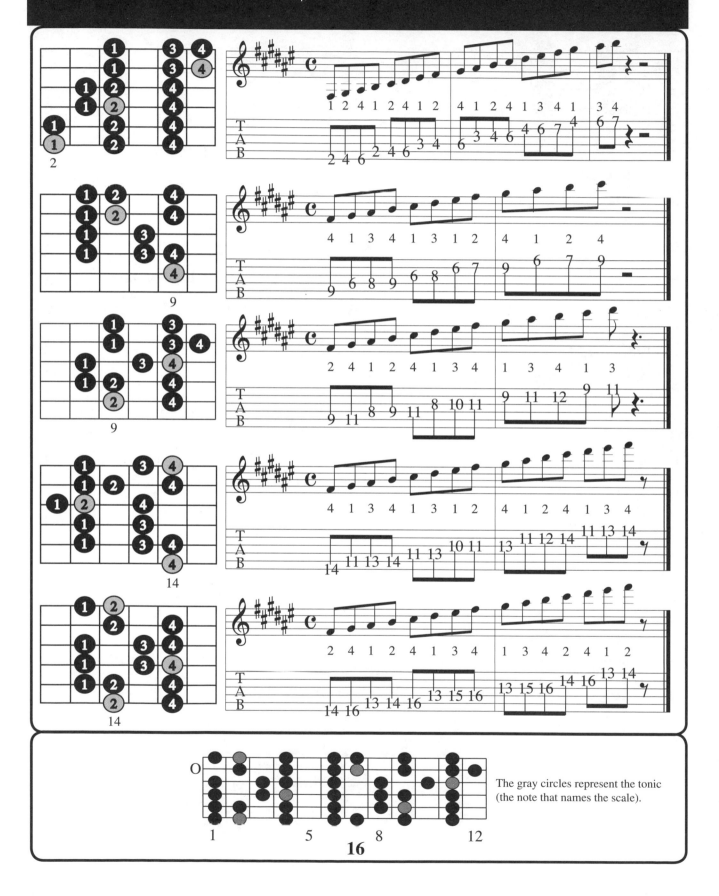

The gray circles represent the tonic (the note that names the scale).

G MAJOR

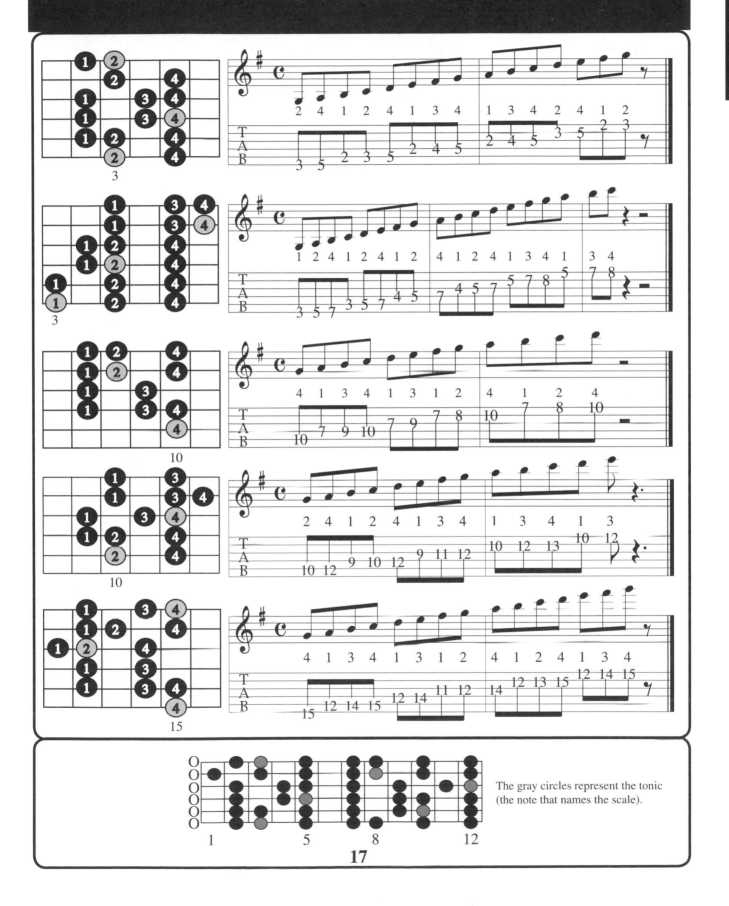

The gray circles represent the tonic
(the note that names the scale).

Ab MAJOR

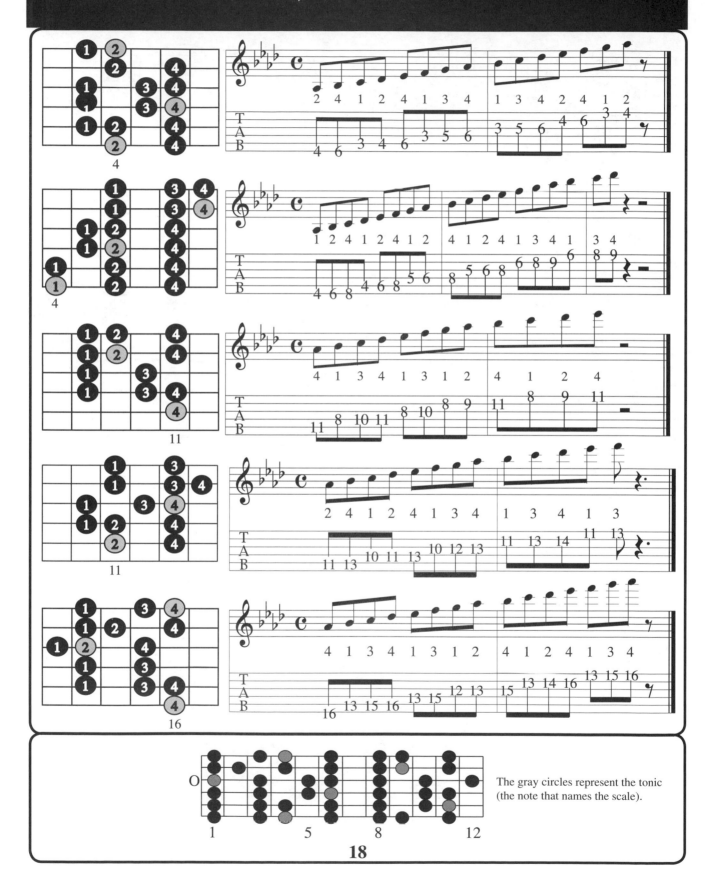

The gray circles represent the tonic (the note that names the scale).

3 NOTES PER STRING MAJOR SCALES

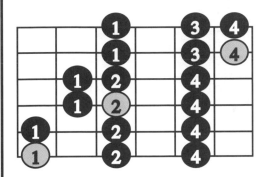
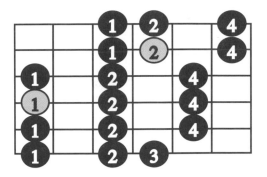

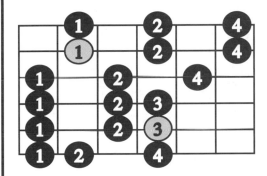
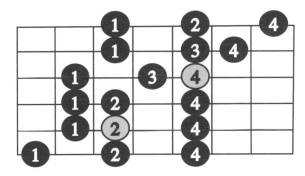

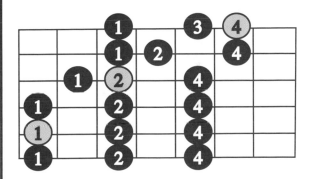
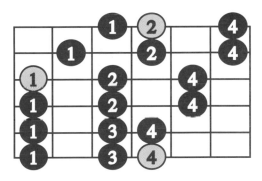

These are the major scales using three notes per string. "Three notes per string" is a concept that allows for fast, fluid playing. Instead of some strings having only two notes and others having three, this scale stays consistent. Hammer-ons and pull-offs also become faster and more fluid using these shapes. When you want speed, try using three notes per string. When the hand is spread out between 5 frets, try the 1, 2, and 4 fingers. They are more independent and, therefore, quicker and more fluid. When spread between 4 frets, fingering becomes more optional, especially when using fingers 1, 3, and 4. You may want to try 1, 2, and 3. This is based on personal preference. Try all options but use logic and consistency to develop good muscle memory.

GENERIC MAJOR SCALES

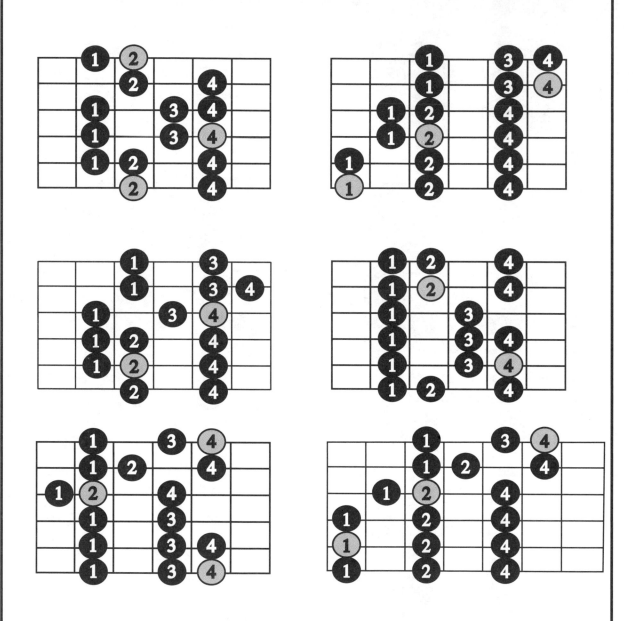

These scales have been called generic shapes for lack of a better name. Previously, diatonic scales have been shown starting from their tonic or root. The scales on this page may start on notes below the tonic. They are generic in that they can be used for major, minor, or modes just by changing what is perceived to be the tonic. In this case, the root or tonic is a major scale.

THE MINOR DIATONIC SCALES

Scale Degrees:	1	2	♭3	4	5	♭6	♭7	(8)
Intervals:		whole step	half step	whole step	whole step	half step	whole step	whole step

Example:
A minor

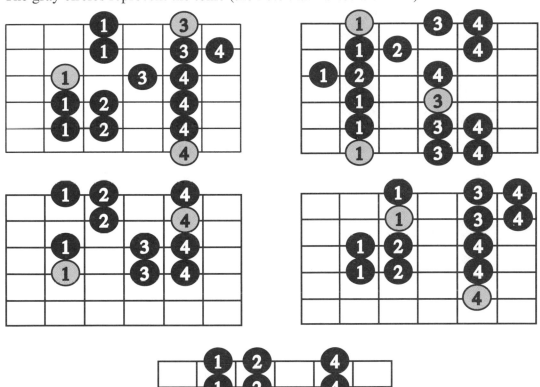

MINOR SCALE PATTERNS

The gray circles represent the tonic (the note that names the scale).

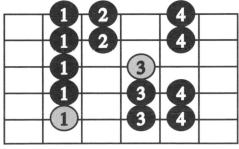

The minor scale is a seven-note scale. All of the other scales will use the major and minor scales for comparison.

Suggestions for usage: Primarily used over minor chords and tunes in a minor keys. May be used over any type of music.

Example: A minor scale over Am7. Try A minor over track 4 of the *Let's Jam! CD Blues & Rock*.

A MINOR

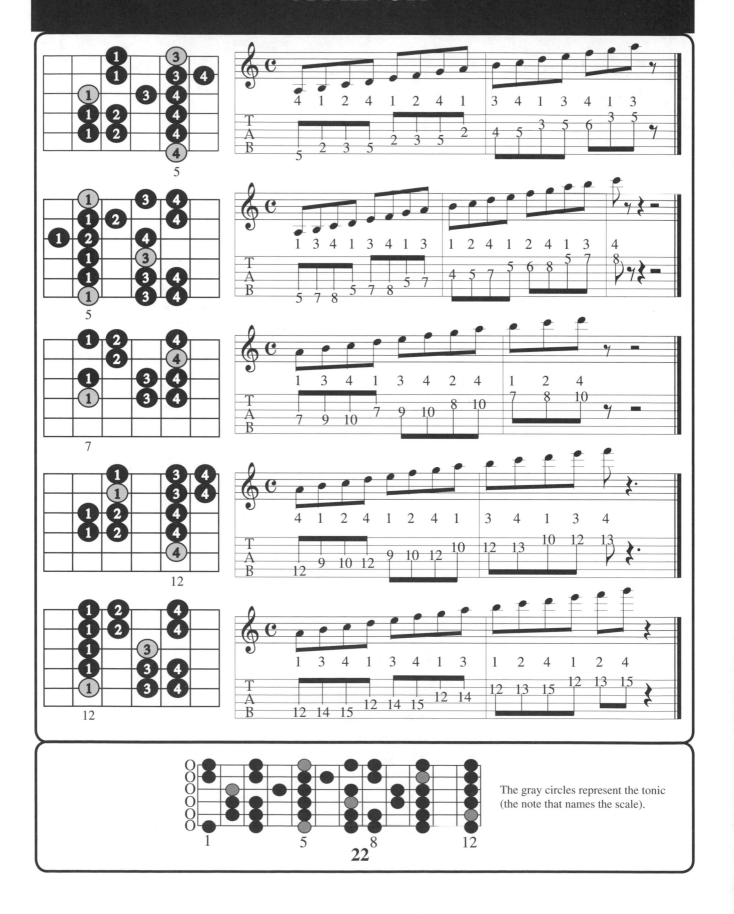

The gray circles represent the tonic (the note that names the scale).

22

B♭ MINOR

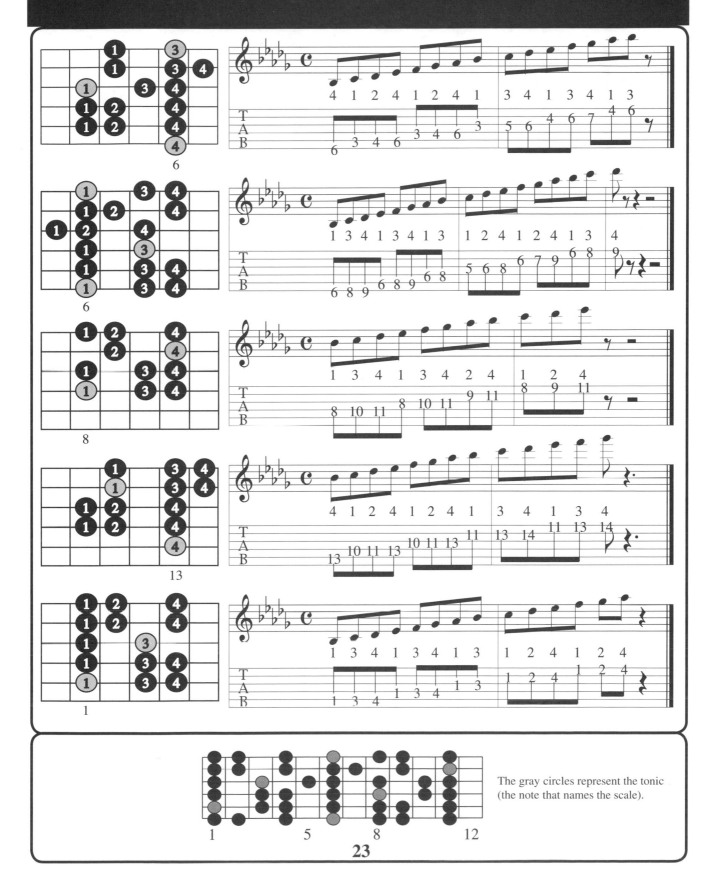

The gray circles represent the tonic (the note that names the scale).

23

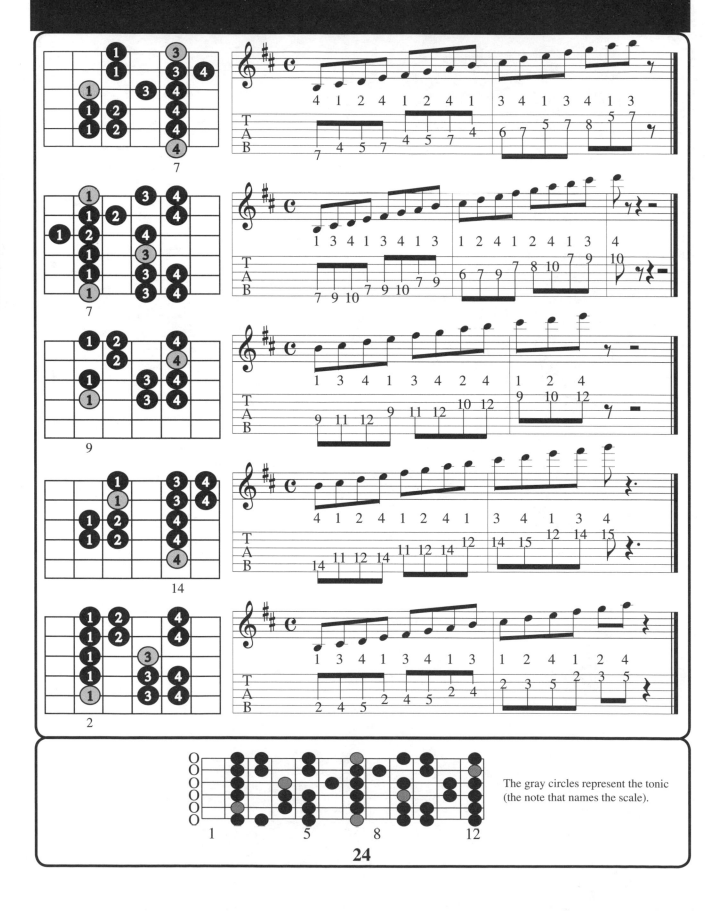

The gray circles represent the tonic (the note that names the scale).

C MINOR

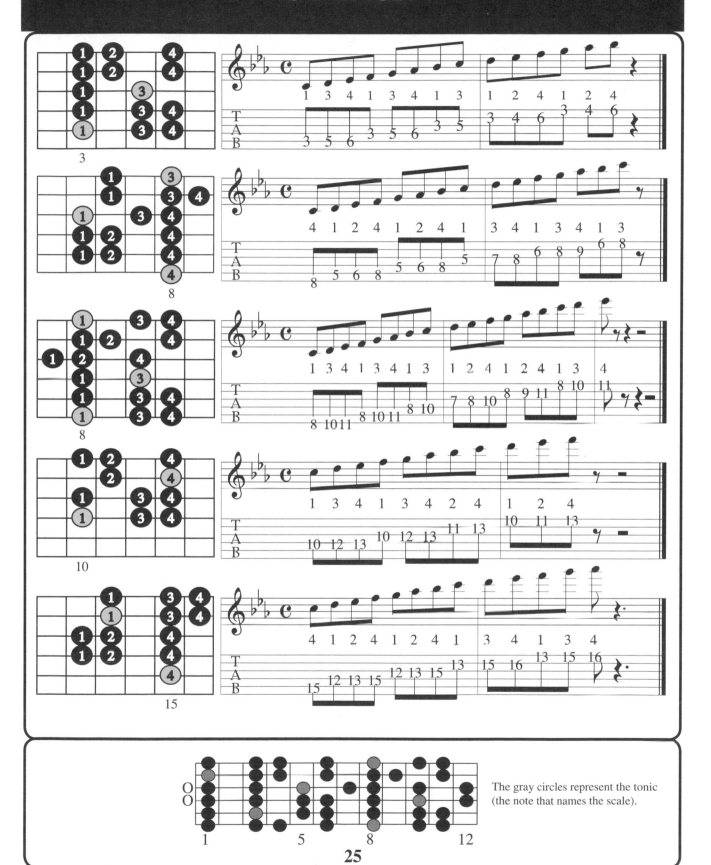

The gray circles represent the tonic (the note that names the scale).

25

C# MINOR

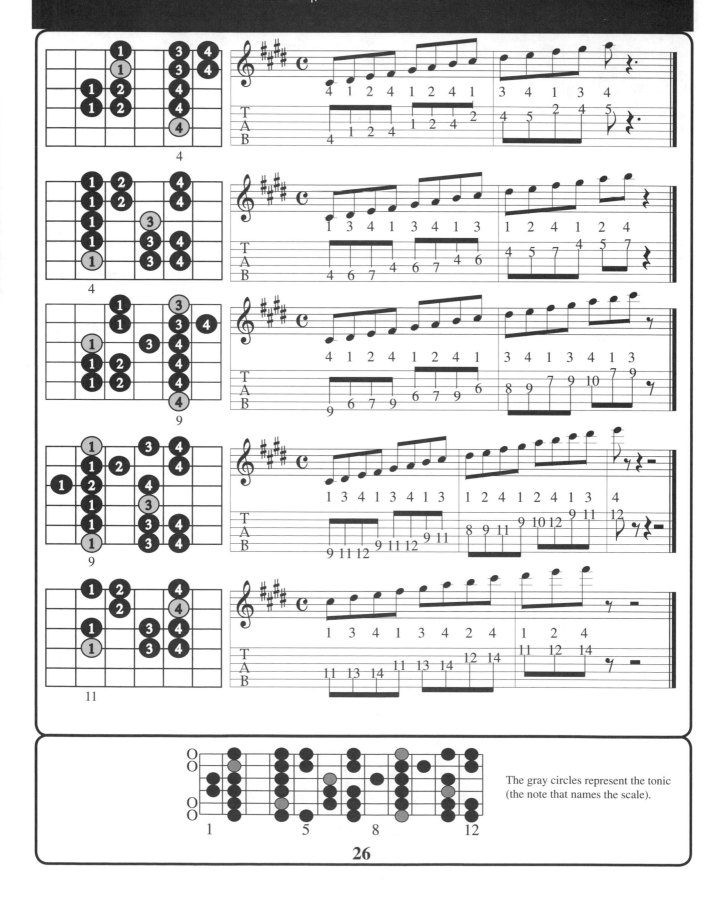

The gray circles represent the tonic (the note that names the scale).

26

D MINOR

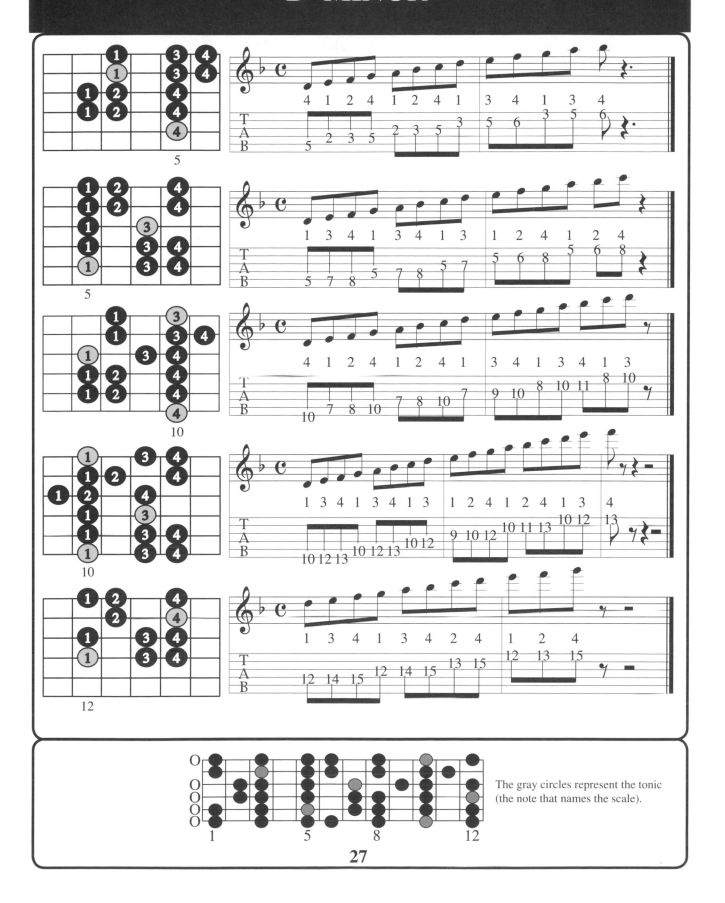

The gray circles represent the tonic (the note that names the scale).

27

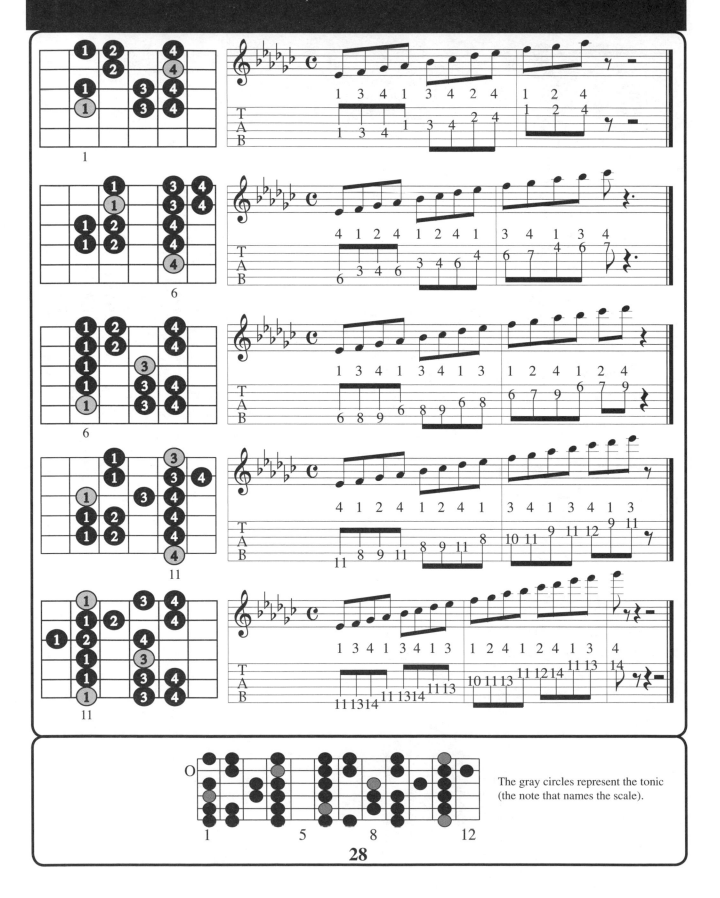

The gray circles represent the tonic (the note that names the scale).

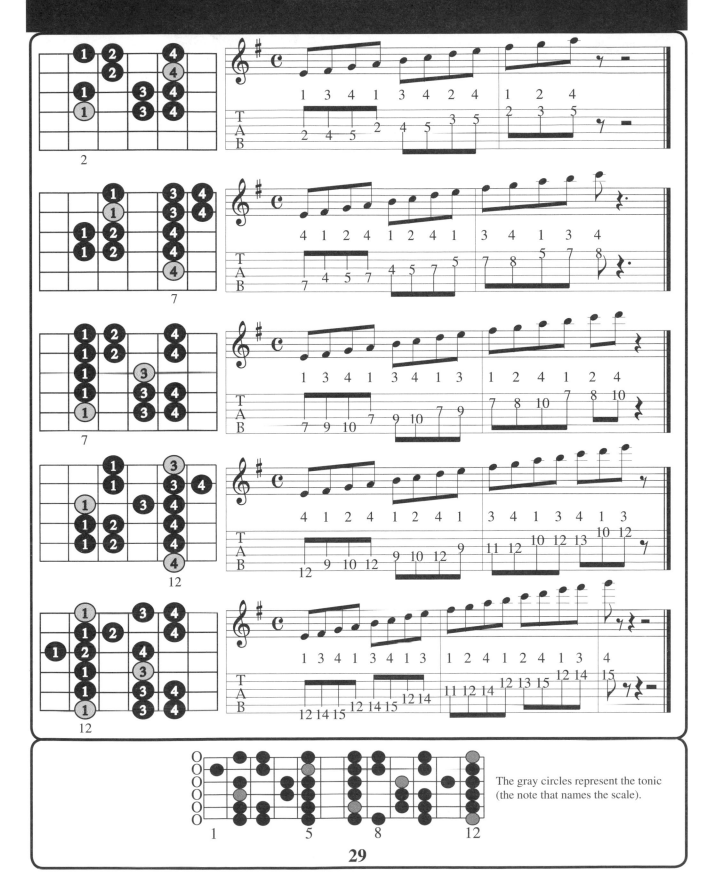

The gray circles represent the tonic (the note that names the scale).

F MINOR

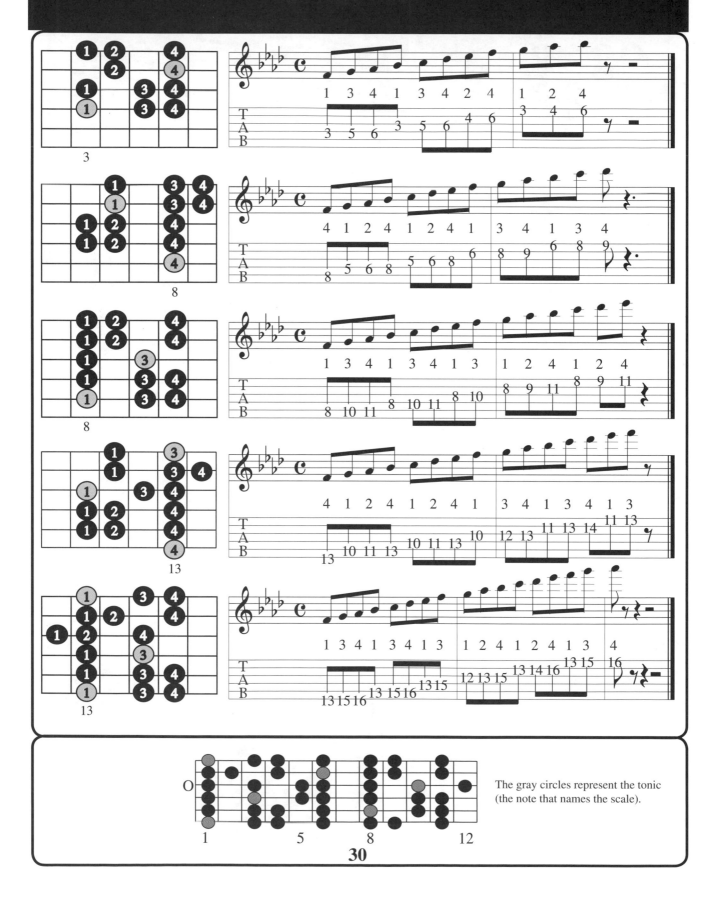

The gray circles represent the tonic (the note that names the scale).

30

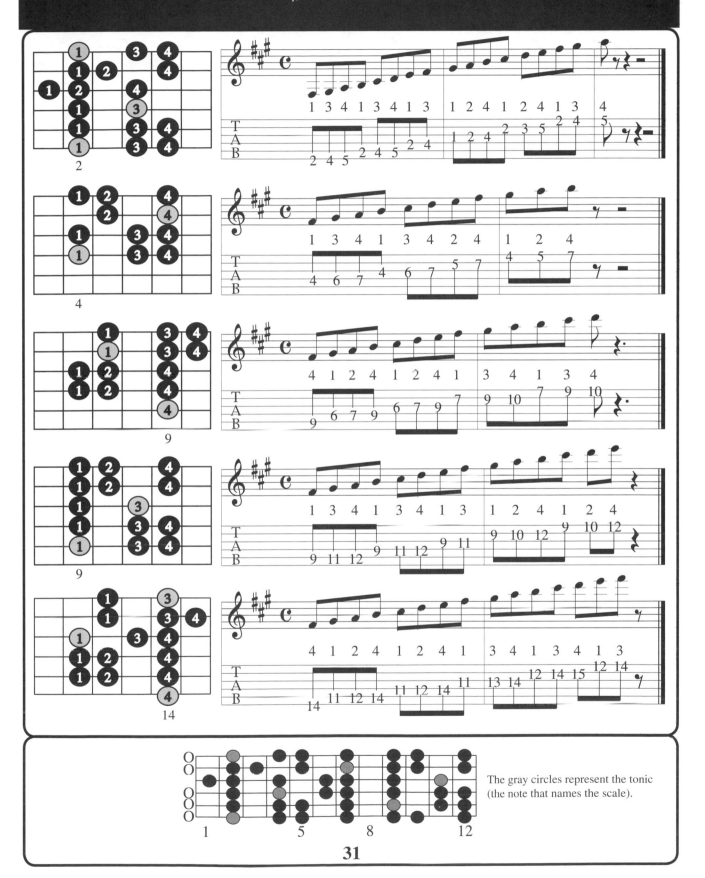

The gray circles represent the tonic (the note that names the scale).

F#
MINOR
.

G MINOR

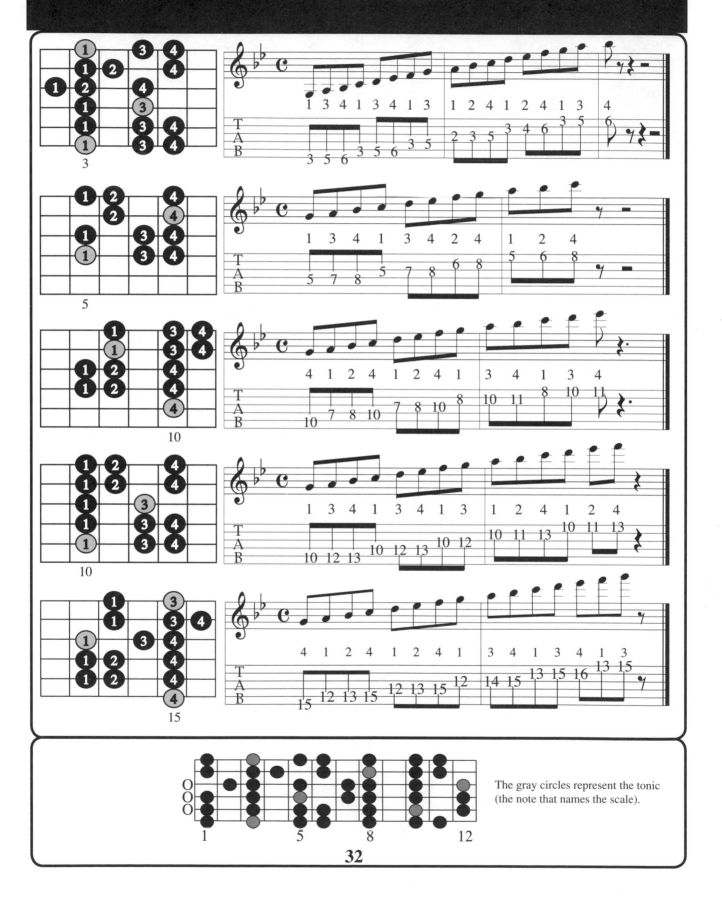

The gray circles represent the tonic (the note that names the scale).

32

A♭ MINOR

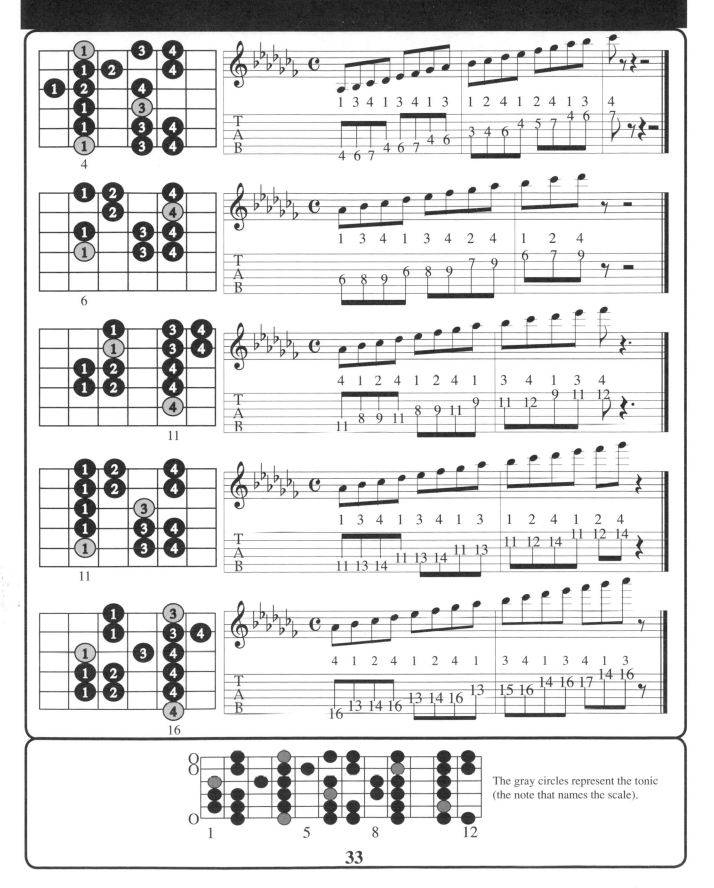

The gray circles represent the tonic (the note that names the scale).

33

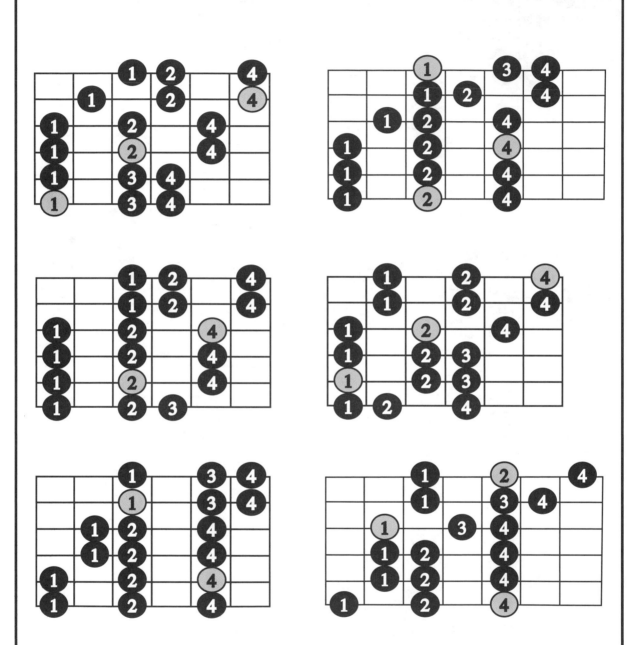

These are minor scales using three notes per string. "Three notes per string" is a concept that allows for fast, fluid playing. Instead of some strings having only two notes and others having three, this scale stays consistent. Hammer-ons and pull-offs also become faster and more fluid. When you want speed, try using three notes per string. When the hand is spread out between five frets, try the 1, 2, and 4 fingers. They are more independent and, therefore, quicker and more fluid. When spread between four frets, fingerings become more optional, especially when using 1, 3, and 4. You may want to try 1, 2, and 3. This is based on personal preference. Try all options, but use logic and consistency to develop good muscle memory.

GENERIC MINOR SCALES

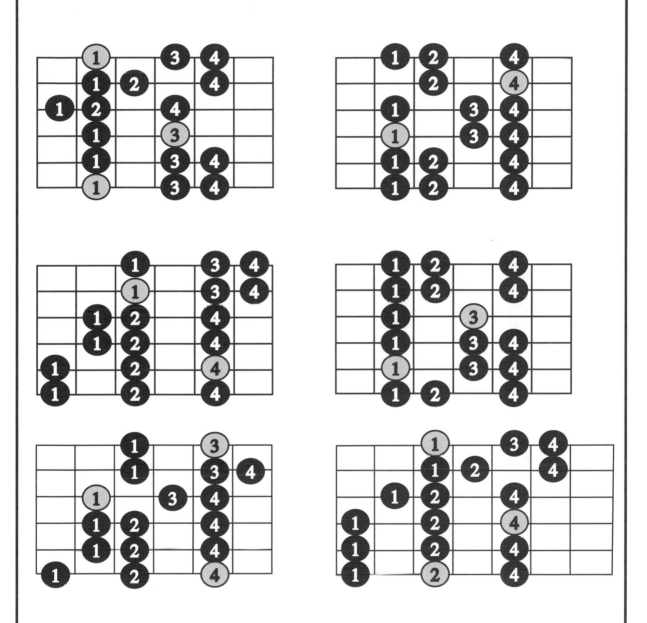

These scales have been called generic shapes for lack of a better name. Previous minor scales have been shown starting from their tonic or root. These scales are shapes that sometimes start on notes below the root. They are generic in that they can be used for major, minor, or modes just by changing what note you consider to be the tonic. In this case, the root or tonic is based on this being a minor scale.

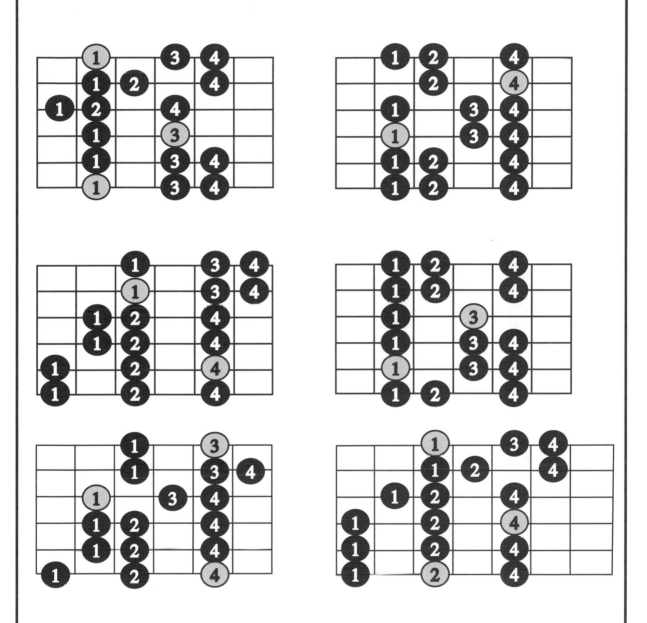

MINOR

35

THE HARMONIC MINOR SCALE

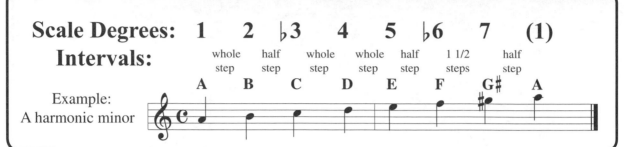

Scale Degrees:	1	2	♭3	4	5	♭6	7	(1)
Intervals:		whole step	half step	whole step	whole step	half step	1 1/2 steps	half step

Example:
A harmonic minor

A B C D E F G# A

HARMONIC MINOR SCALE PATTERNS

The gray circles represent the tonic (the note that names the scale).

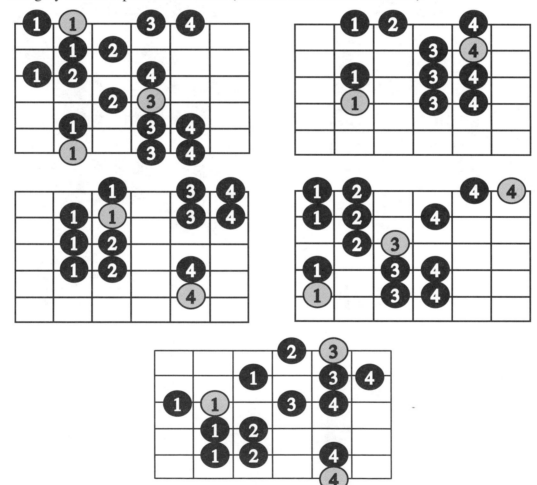

The harmonic minor scale is a seven-note scale. It is a variation of the natural minor scale. Instead of a flat seven, which is in the natural minor scale, the harmonic minor scale raises the seventh a half step. The raised seventh degree gives this scale a very distinct sound.

Suggestions for usage: Primarily used over minor chords and over certain chord progressions including the raised seventh degree. Try this scale over jazz, blues, rock, etc.

Example: A harmonic minor scale over Am7 or over Am7 E7. (E7 would contain the raised seventh degree, G#)

36

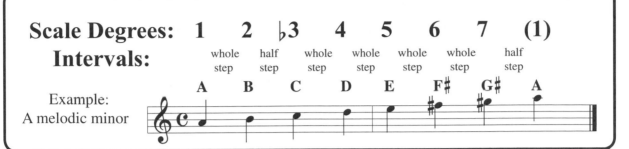

Scale Degrees:	1	2	♭3	4	5	6	7	(1)
Intervals:		whole step	half step	whole step	whole step	whole step	whole step	half step

Example:
A melodic minor

A B C D E F# G# A

MELODIC MINOR SCALE PATTERNS

The gray circles represent the tonic (the note that names the scale).

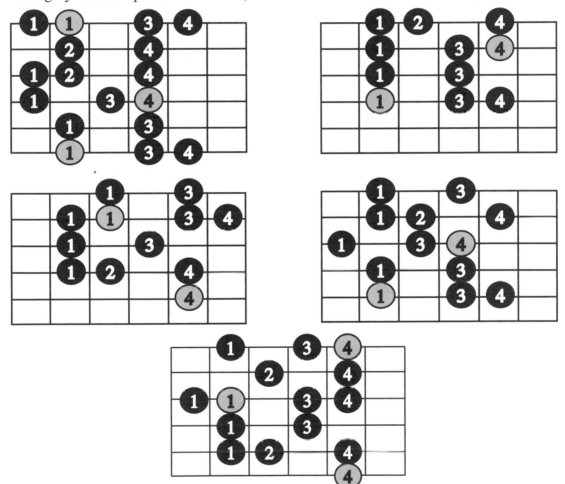

The melodic minor scale is a seven-note scale. It is a natural minor scale with a raised sixth and seventh degree. Melodic minor is used in a variety of ways in all genres of music.

Suggestions for usage: Primarily used over minor chords, it also sounds great over a dominant four chord in the same key. Modes of this scale are used as well. Playing this scale a half step higher than usual over a dominant five chord gives you the altered dominant scale. (Example: F melodic minor over E7 resolving on an A chord)

Example: A melodic minor scale over Am. A melodic minor also sounds good over D9. A# melodic minor is the altered dominant scale over D7. Try B melodic minor over track 10 and 11 of the *Let's Jam! CD Blues & Rock*.

MELODIC MINOR

RELATIVE MAJOR AND MINOR

WHAT IS RELATIVE MAJOR AND MINOR
OR
THE AEOLIAN RELATIONSHIP

Understanding relative major and minor is a very important concept that will improve your knowledge and use of scales. Here is the concept of relative major and minor, also called "the aeolian relationship":

For every major scale there is a minor scale with exactly the same notes.

For example: C major has exactly the same notes as A minor, and G major has exactly the same notes as E minor. This means when you learn the C major scale, you know the A minor scale as well. When you learn the G major scale, you know the E minor scale as well. Let's examine this further. Here are the notes to C major and A minor

C major	C D E F G A B C
A minor	A B C D E F G A

Notice these are both seven-note scales. C major starts on the note C, and A minor starts on the note A, but otherwise they contain the same set of notes. This is the concept of relative major and minor. C major is related to A minor and A minor is related to C major. The same is true for G major and E minor. G major and E minor contain the same set of notes. Here are these two scales:

G major	G A B C D E F♯ G
E minor	E F♯ G A B C D E

HOW TO FIND RELATIVE MAJOR AND MINOR SCALES

Relative major and minor scales are a third or three half steps apart. Let's use C major as an example. Take the note C of the C major scale and go down three half steps and you arrive on the note A. Another way of looking at this is to take the note C and go down three notes of the scale: C - B - A. You arrive on the note A, which is the relative minor scale.

If you are starting from the A minor scale, go up three half steps and you arrive on the note C, and you have found the relative major scale to A minor.

Here's one last way of finding related major and minor scales. The relative minor always starts on the 6th degree of the major scale.

$$\text{C D E F G \textcircled{A} B C}$$
$$\text{1 2 3 4 5 \textcircled{6} 7 8}$$

The relative major always starts on the 3rd degree of the minor scale.

$$\text{A B \textcircled{C} D E F G A}$$
$$\text{1 2 \textcircled{3} 4 5 6 7 8}$$

So what does all this mean to you? For soloing or improvising purposes, C major is the same as A minor. Relative major and minor scales have the same notes, so you may use whichever of the two you prefer. *You may also use the same fingerings for both scales*. One word of caution: when playing in C major, the notes that are emphasized are different than in A minor. This becomes especially important on the ending notes of a phrase. The first degree and fifth degree of either scale are usually emphasized more than the others. In C, this would mean the notes C and G. In A minor, this would mean the notes A and E. Your ear should help you in this regard.

Here is a chart of the relative major and minor scales. It would be wise to memorize this chart.

RELATIVE MAJOR AND MINOR

A Major	F♯ Minor
B♭ Major	G Minor
B Major	G♯ Minor
C Major	A Minor
C♯ Major	A♯ Minor
D Major	B Minor
E♭ Major	C Minor
E Major	C♯ Minor
F Major	D Minor
F♯ Major	D♯ Minor
G Major	E Minor
A♭ Major	F Minor

Scale Degrees:	1	2	3	5	6	(8)
Intervals:		whole step	whole step	1 1/2 steps	whole step	1 1/2 steps

Example:
C major pentatonic

MAJOR PENTATONIC SCALE PATTERNS

The gray circles represent the tonic (the note that names the scale).

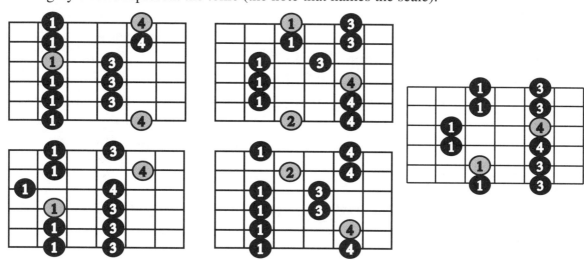

EXTENDED MAJOR PENTATONIC

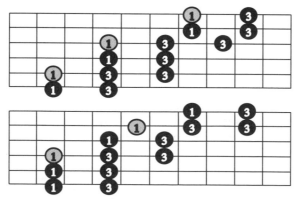

The major pentatonic scale is a five-note scale. I like to think of major pentatonic as a shortened major scale. The two missing notes from the major scale make this scale "always right".

Suggestions for usage: Primarily used over major chords and tunes in major keys. May be used over any type of music.

Example: C major pentatonic scale over a C chord or a song in C major. Try E major pentatonic over track 11 and Bb major pentatonic over track 13 of the *Let's Jam! CD Jazz & Blues*.

A MAJOR PENTATONIC

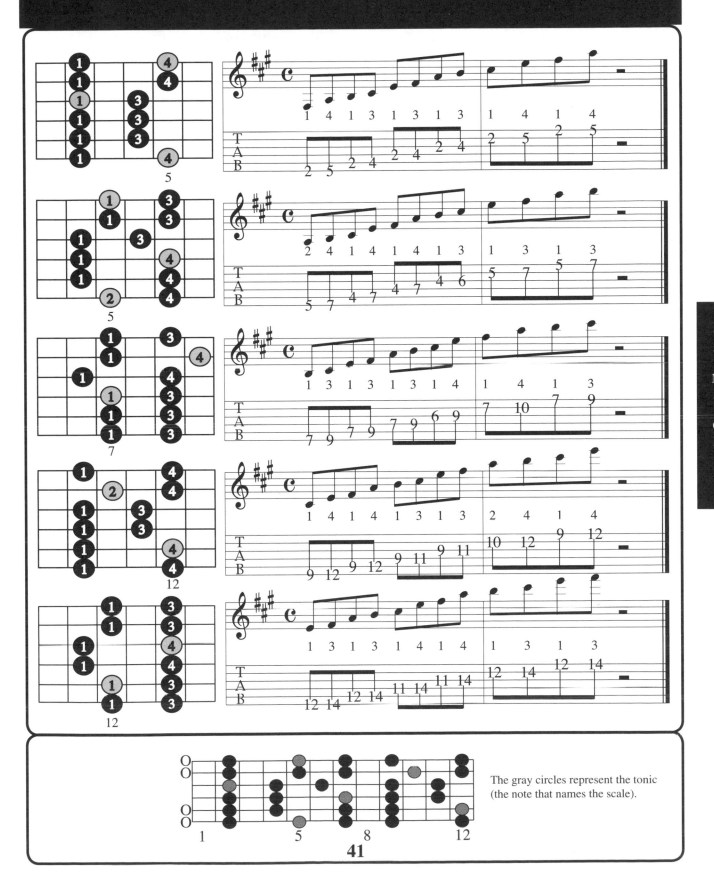

The gray circles represent the tonic (the note that names the scale).

41

B♭ MAJOR PENTATONIC

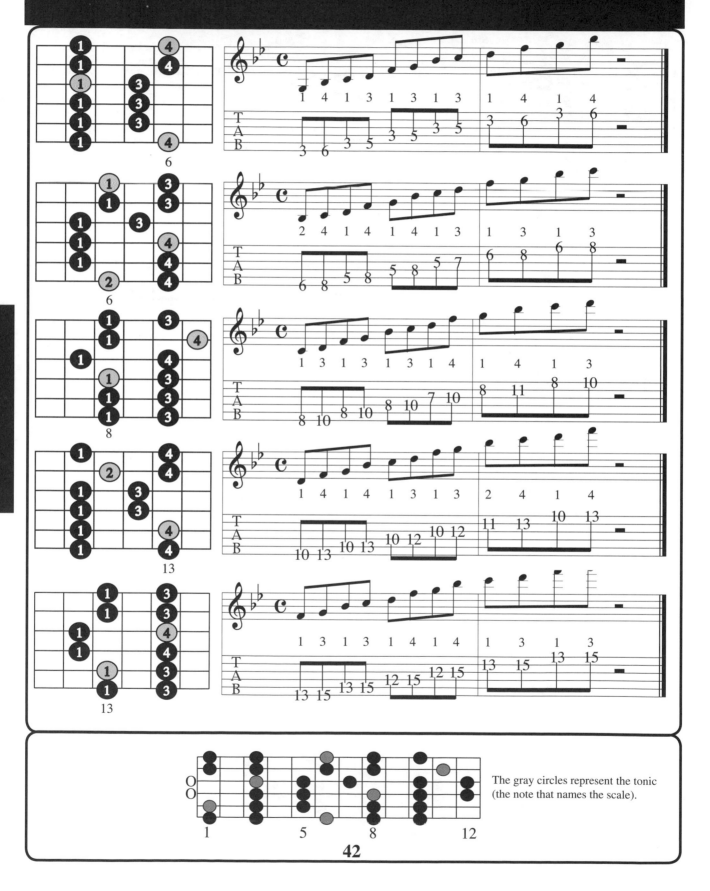

The gray circles represent the tonic (the note that names the scale).

B MAJOR PENTATONIC

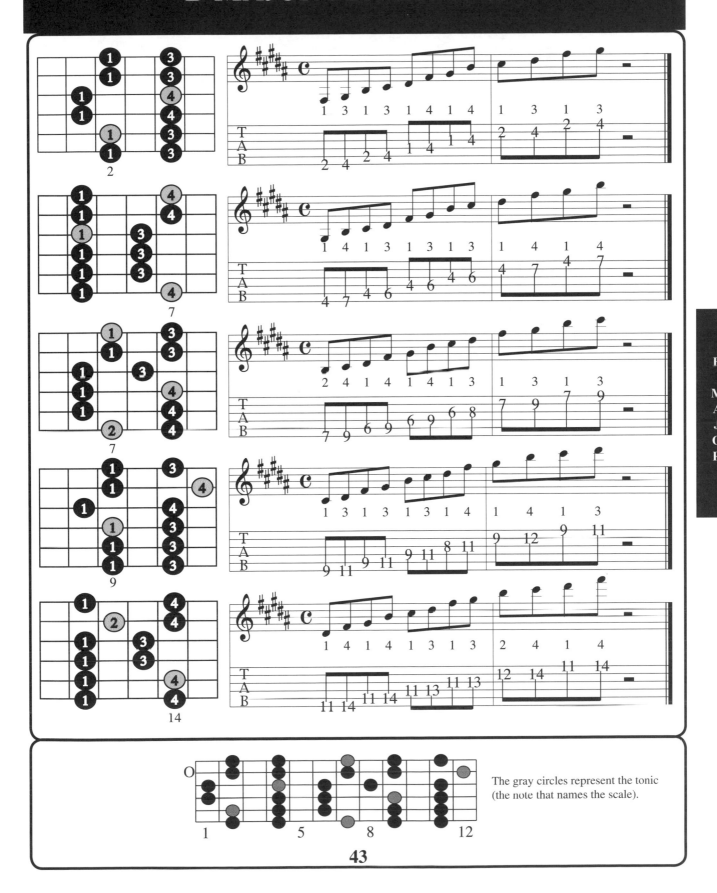

The gray circles represent the tonic (the note that names the scale).

C MAJOR PENTATONIC

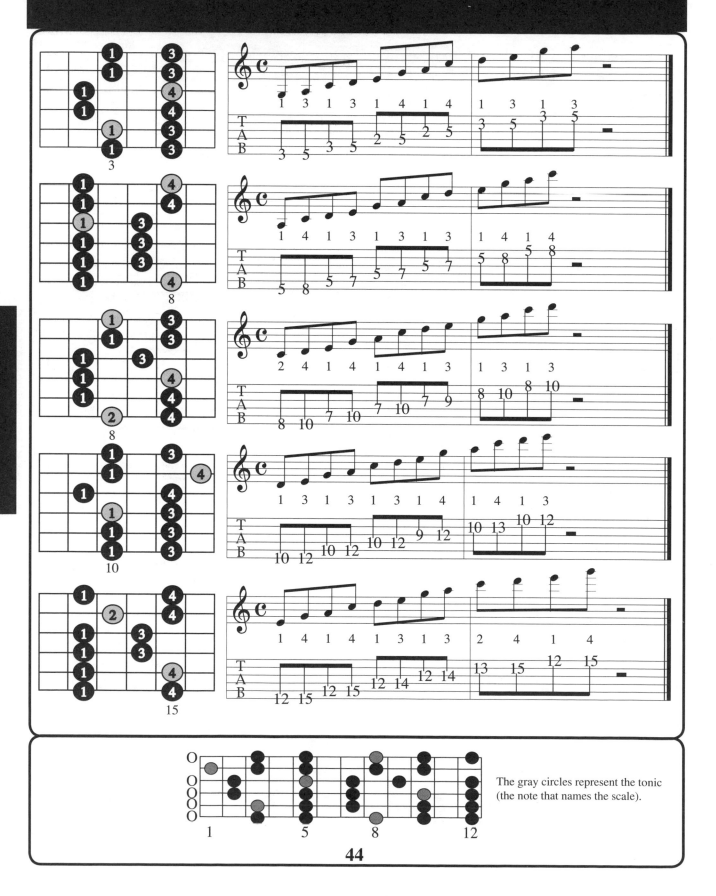

The gray circles represent the tonic (the note that names the scale).

44

C♯ MAJOR PENTATONIC

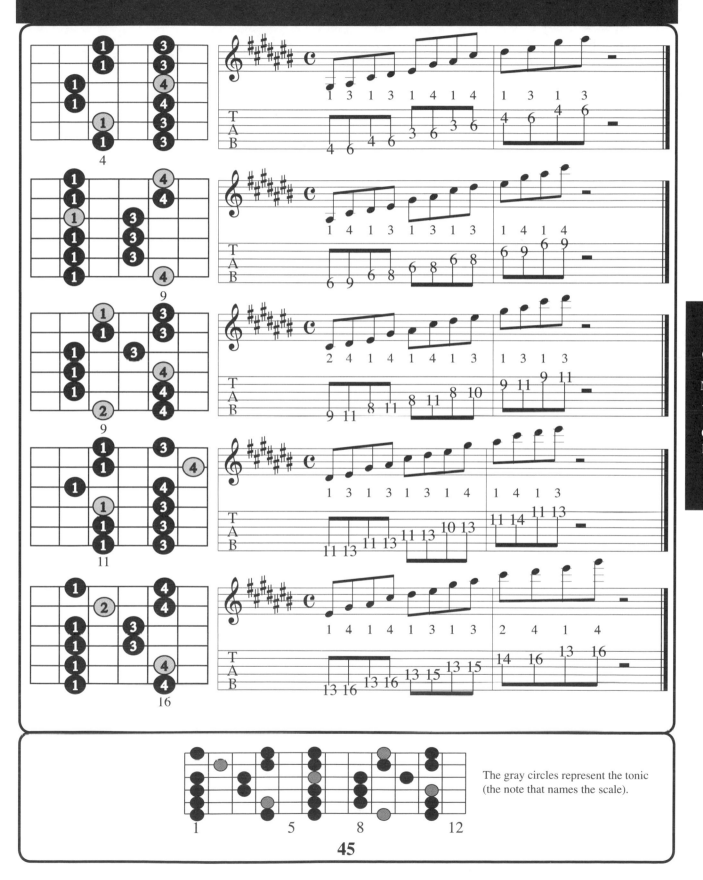

The gray circles represent the tonic (the note that names the scale).

45

D MAJOR PENTATONIC

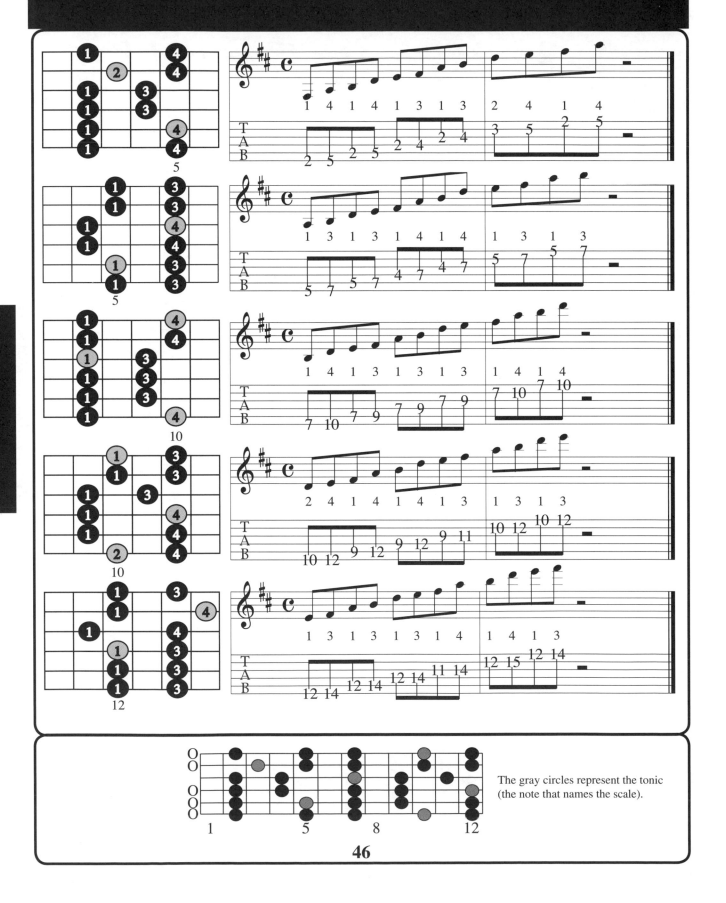

The gray circles represent the tonic (the note that names the scale).

E♭ MAJOR PENTATONIC

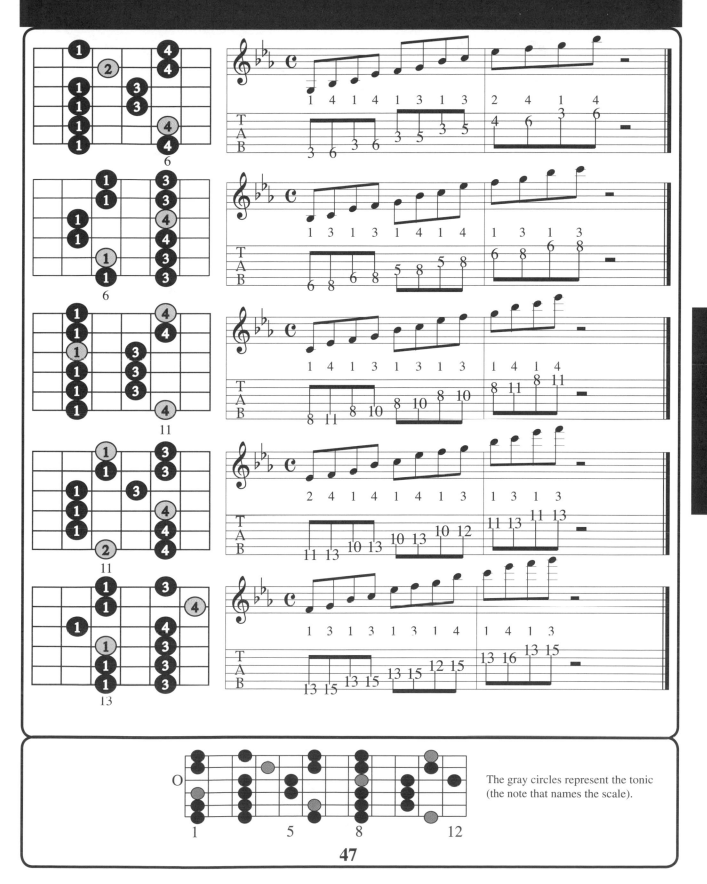

The gray circles represent the tonic (the note that names the scale).

47

E MAJOR PENTATONIC

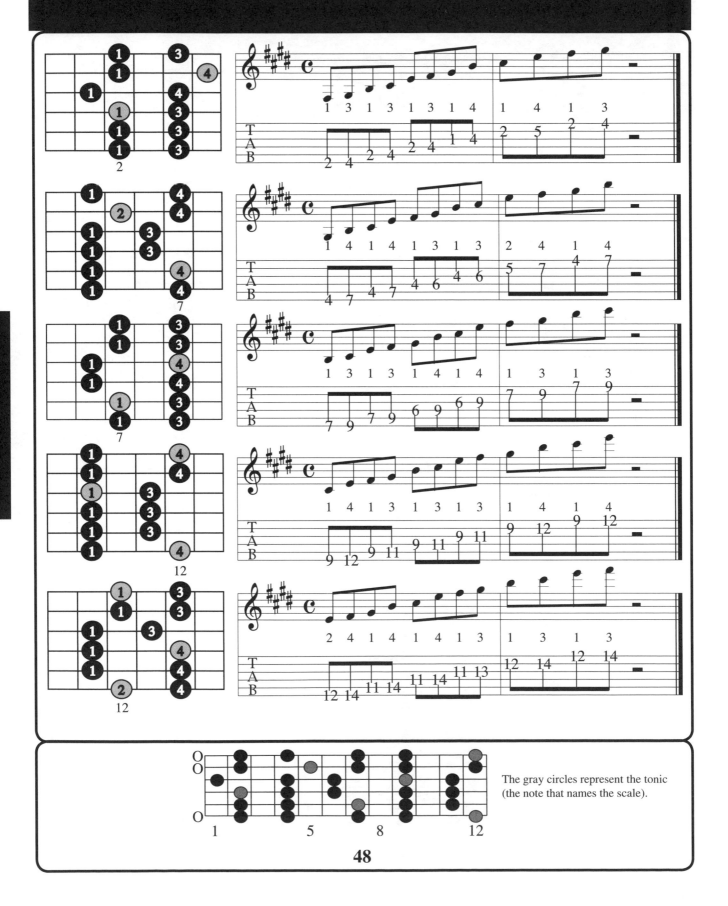

The gray circles represent the tonic (the note that names the scale).

48

F MAJOR PENTATONIC

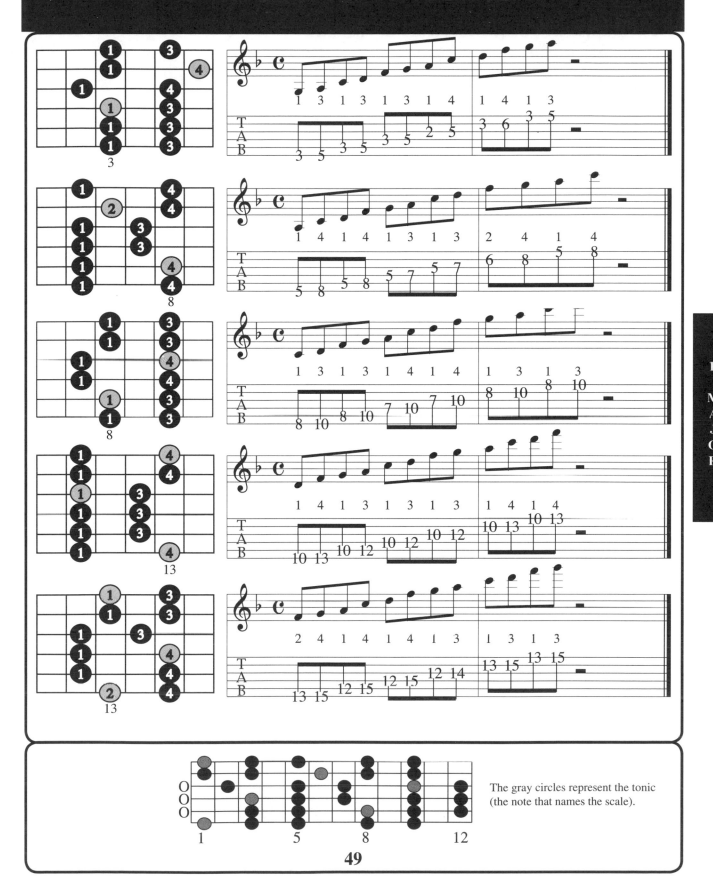

The gray circles represent the tonic (the note that names the scale).

49

F# MAJOR PENTATONIC

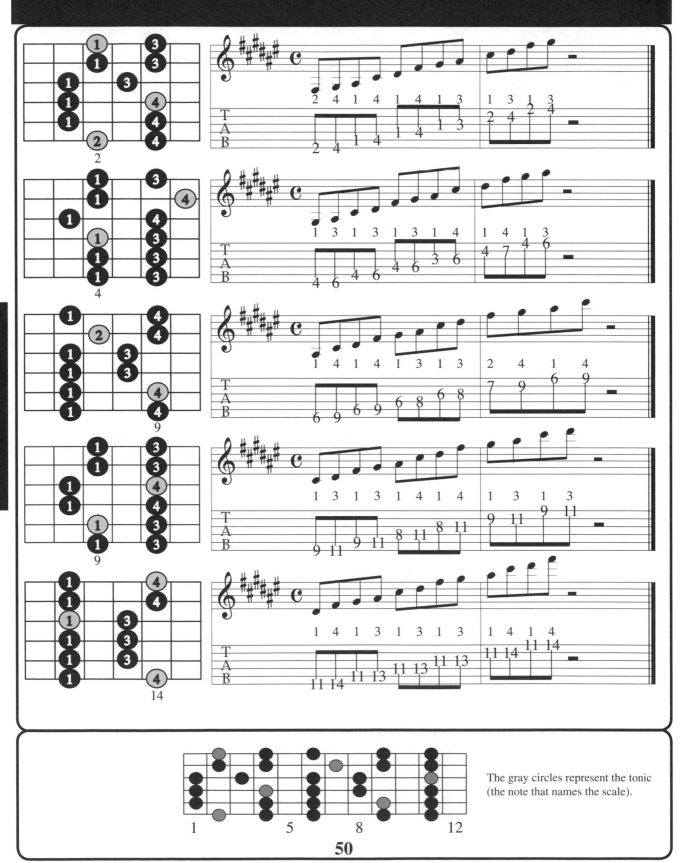

The gray circles represent the tonic (the note that names the scale).

50

G MAJOR PENTATONIC

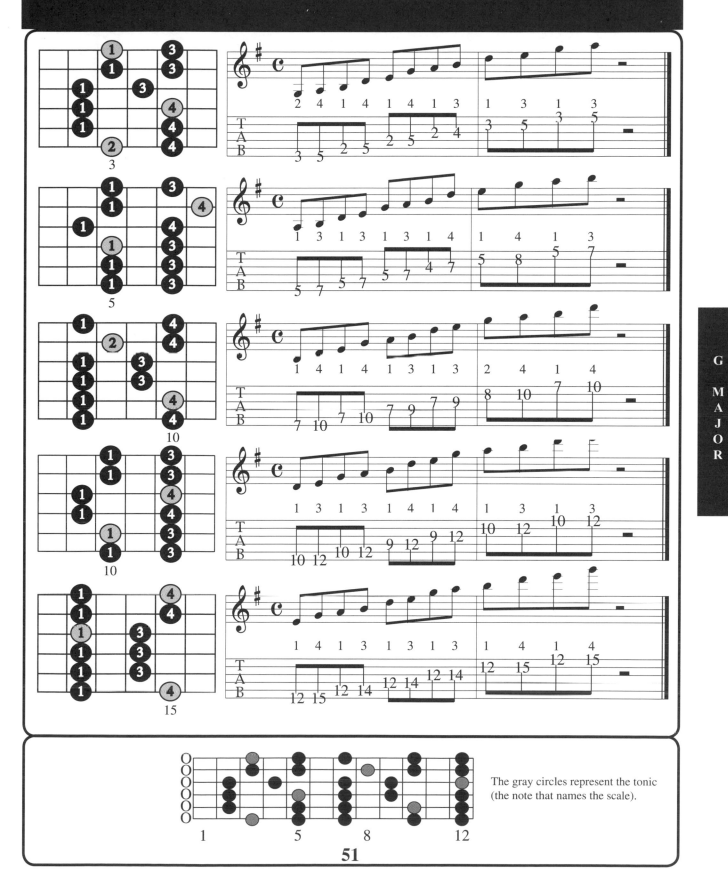

The gray circles represent the tonic (the note that names the scale).

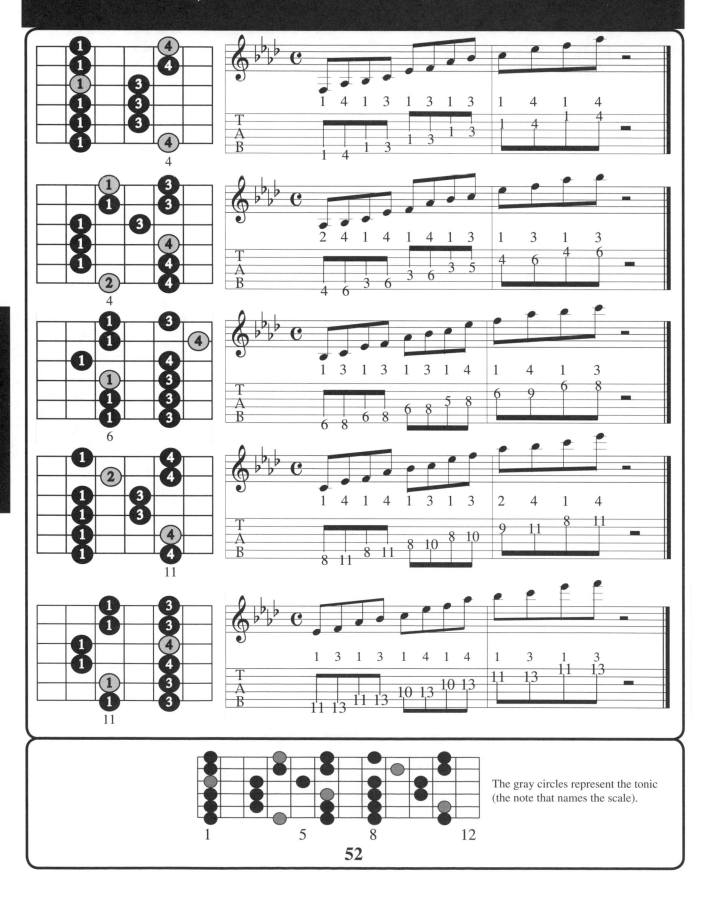

The gray circles represent the tonic (the note that names the scale).

MINOR PENTATONIC SCALES

Scale Degrees:	1	♭3	4	5	♭7	(8)
Intervals:		1 1/2 steps	whole step	whole step	1 1/2 steps	whole step

Example: A minor pentatonic

A   C   D   E   G   A

MINOR PENTATONIC SCALE PATTERNS

The gray circles represent the tonic (the note that names the scale).

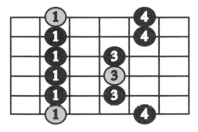

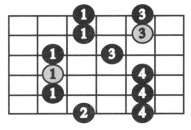

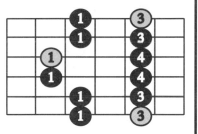

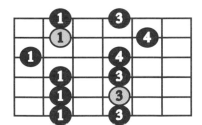

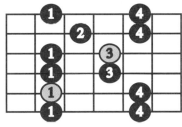

EXTENDED MINOR PENTATONIC

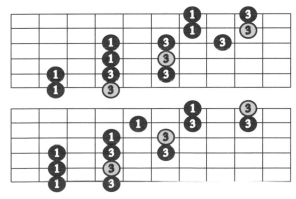

The minor pentatonic scale is a five-note scale. I like to think of minor pentatonic as a shortened minor scale. The two missing notes make minor pentatonic "always right."

Suggestions for usage: Primarily used over minor chords and tunes in minor keys. Also big over blues tunes in major or minor keys. May be used over any type of music.

Example: A minor pentatonic scale over Am7. Try A minor pentatonic over track 4 and 12 of the *Let's Jam! CD Blues & Rock*. Also try C minor pentatonic over track 9 and Gm pentatonic over track 12 of the *Let's Jam! CD Jazz & Blues*.

A MINOR PENTATONIC

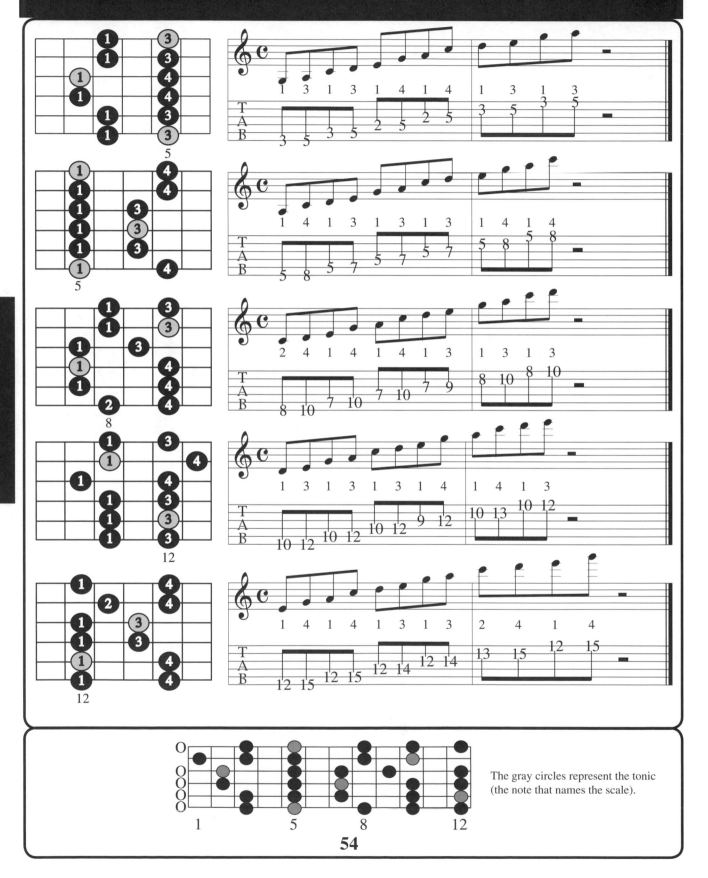

The gray circles represent the tonic (the note that names the scale).

B♭ MINOR PENTATONIC

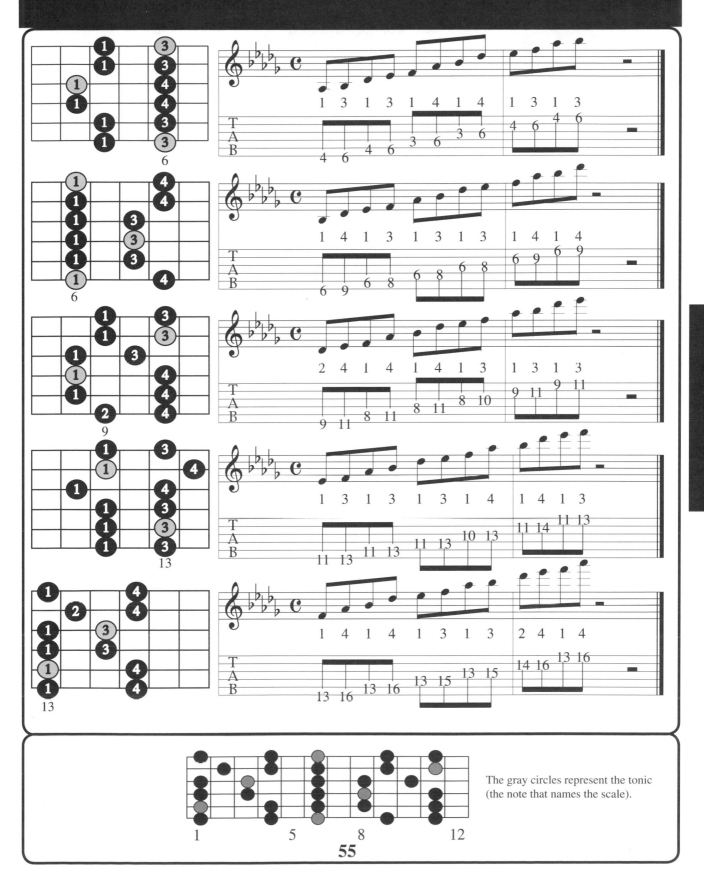

The gray circles represent the tonic (the note that names the scale).

55

B MINOR PENTATONIC

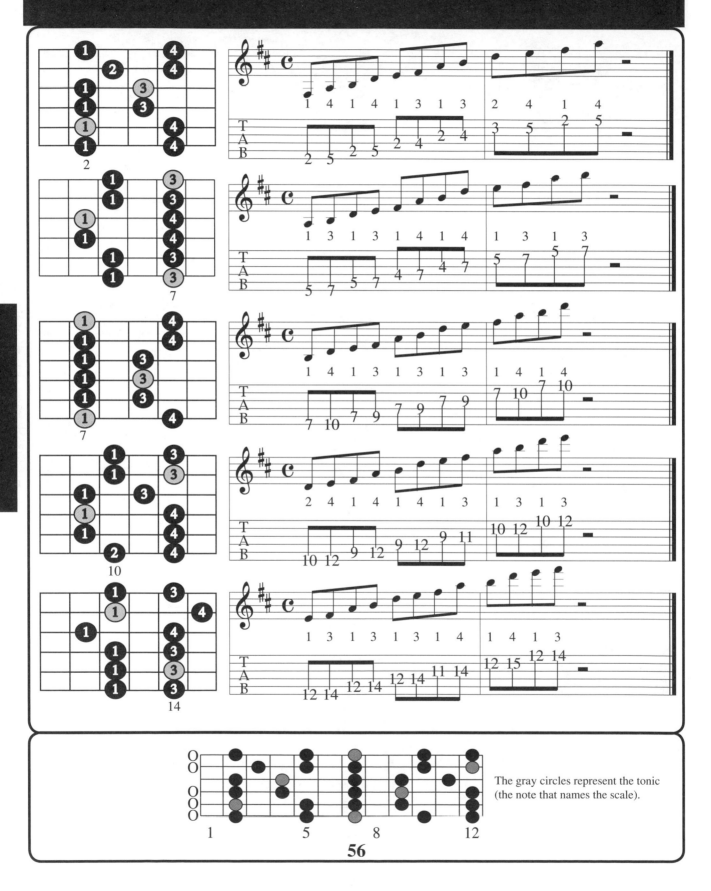

The gray circles represent the tonic
(the note that names the scale).

C MINOR PENTATONIC

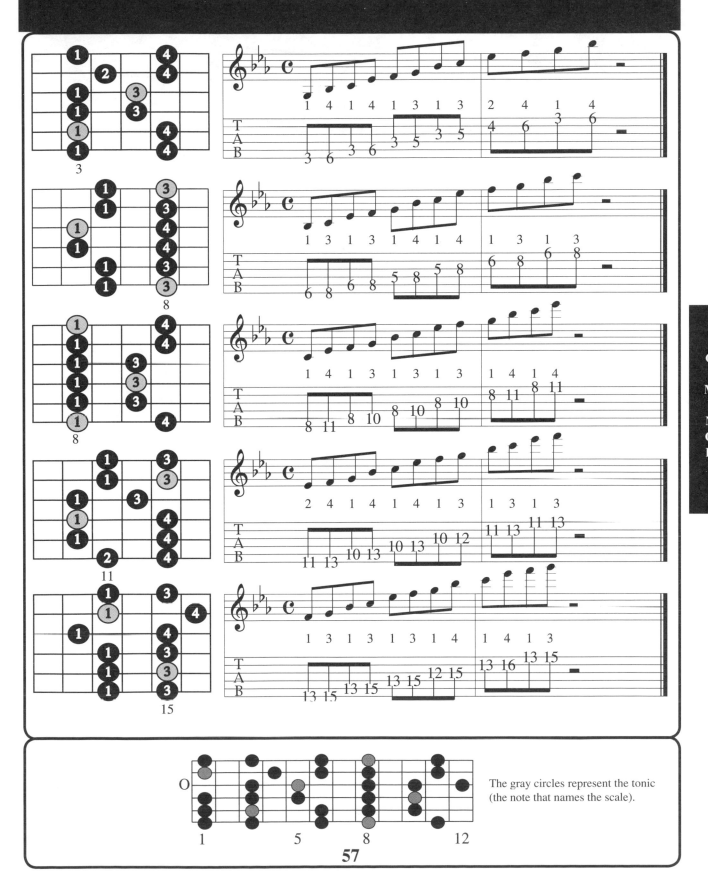

The gray circles represent the tonic (the note that names the scale).

57

C# MINOR PENTATONIC

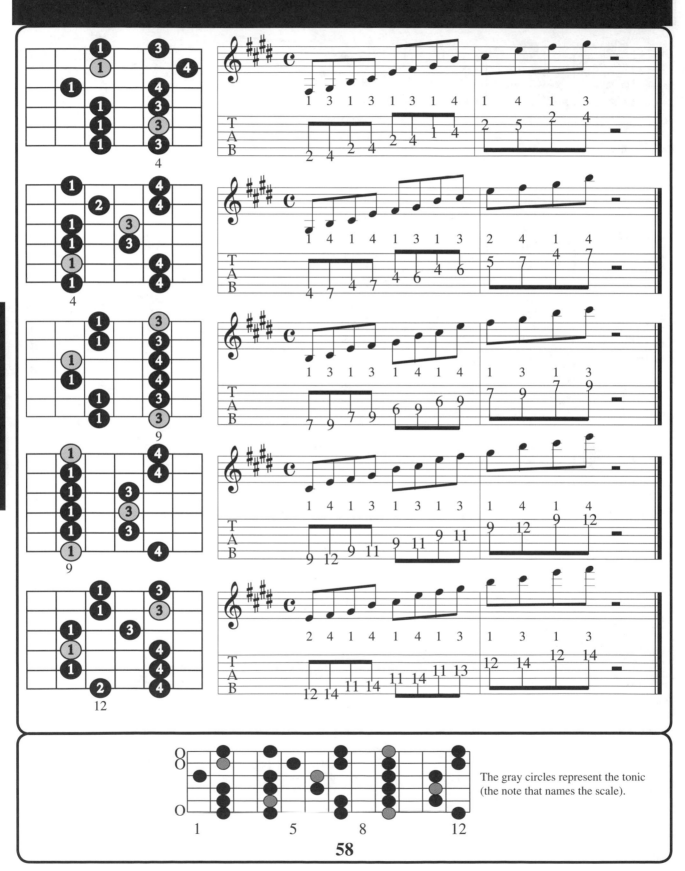

The gray circles represent the tonic (the note that names the scale).

D MINOR PENTATONIC

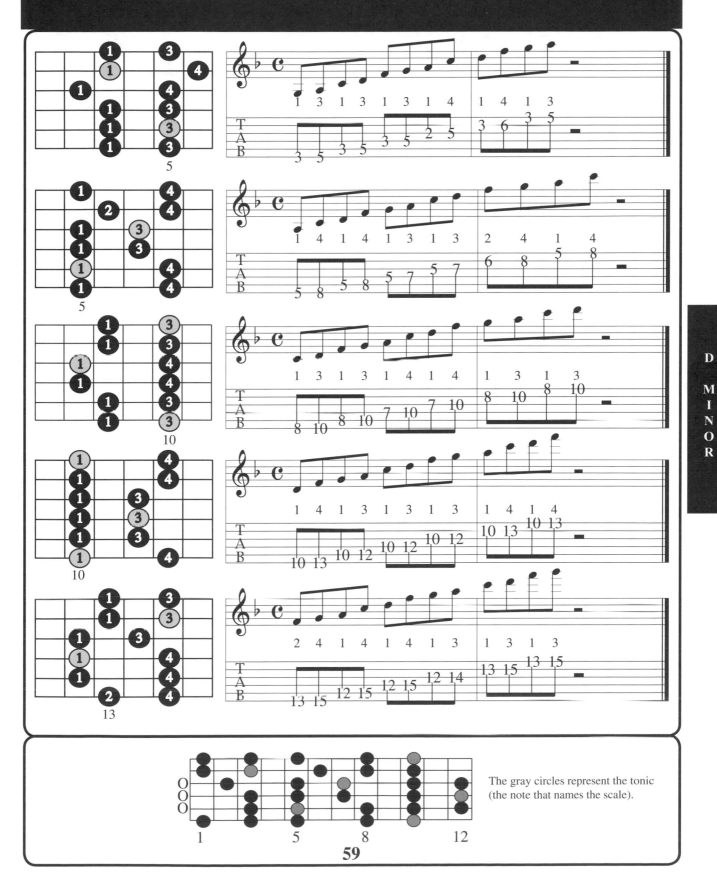

The gray circles represent the tonic (the note that names the scale).

59

E♭ MINOR PENTATONIC

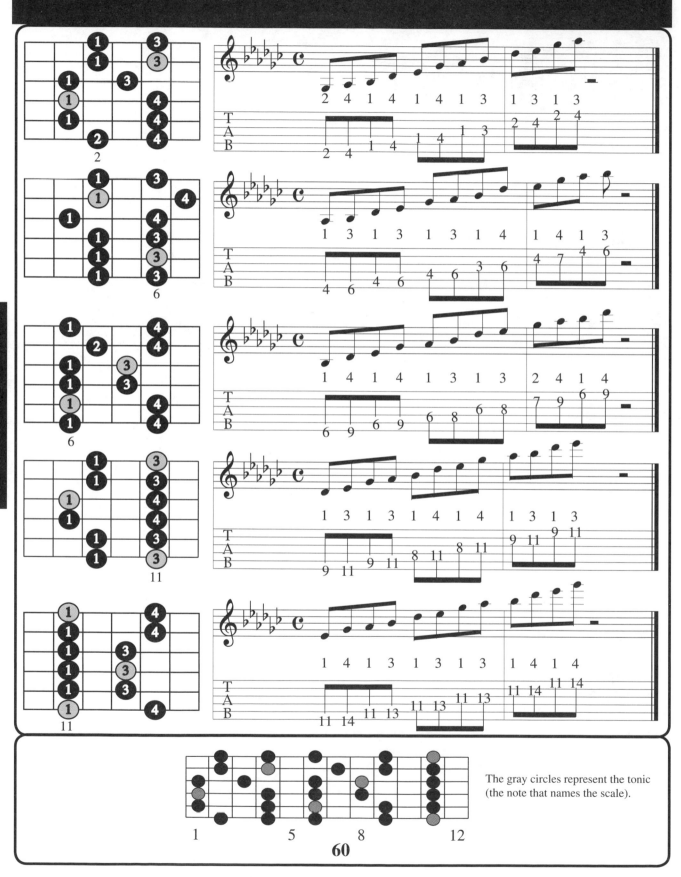

The gray circles represent the tonic (the note that names the scale).

60

E MINOR PENTATONIC

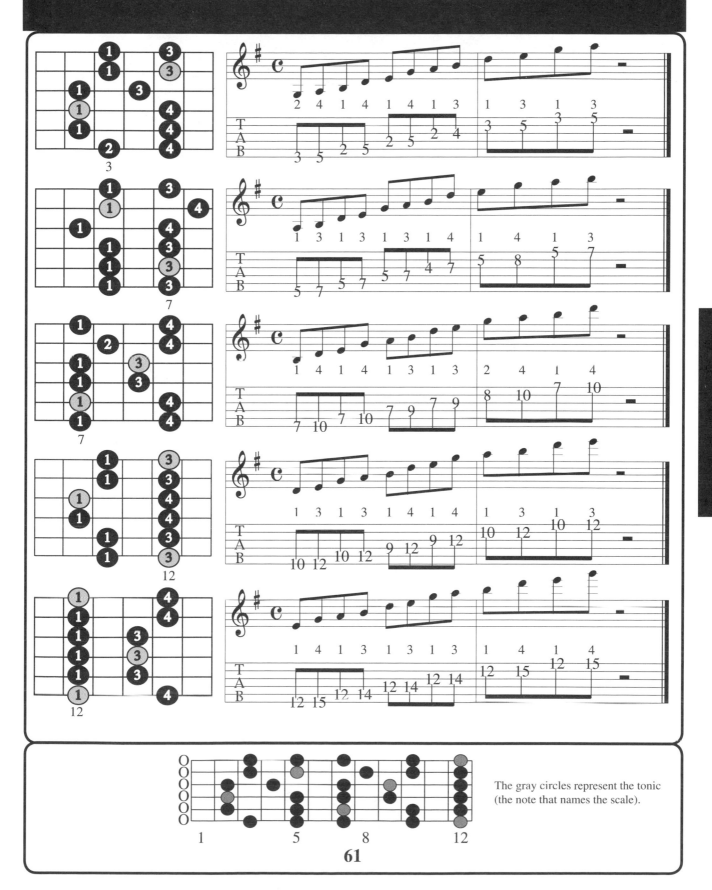

The gray circles represent the tonic (the note that names the scale).

F MINOR PENTATONIC

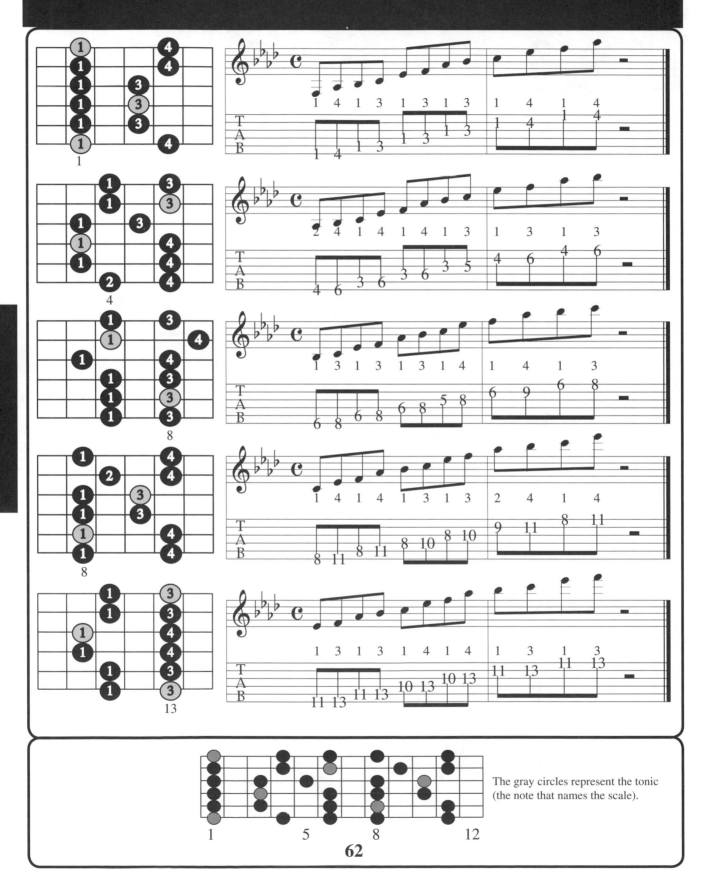

The gray circles represent the tonic (the note that names the scale).

F# MINOR PENTATONIC

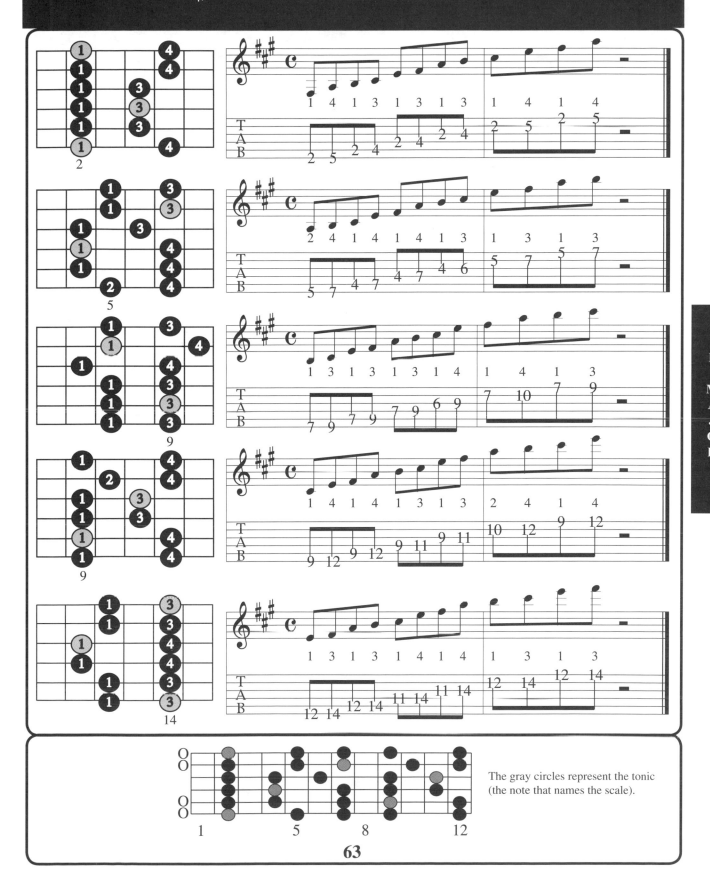

The gray circles represent the tonic (the note that names the scale).

63

G MINOR PENTATONIC

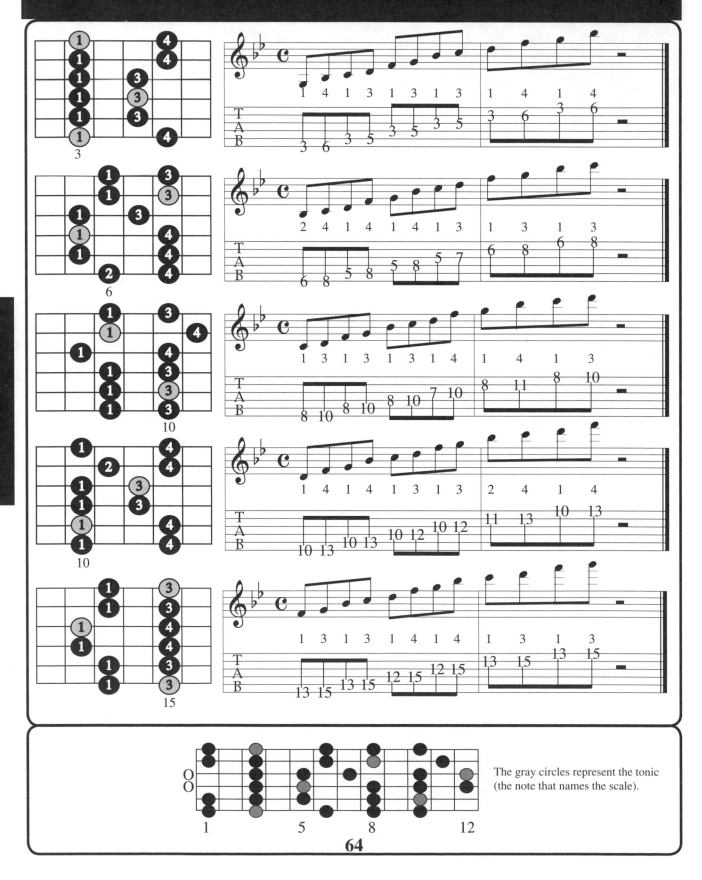

The gray circles represent the tonic (the note that names the scale).

A♭ MINOR PENTATONIC

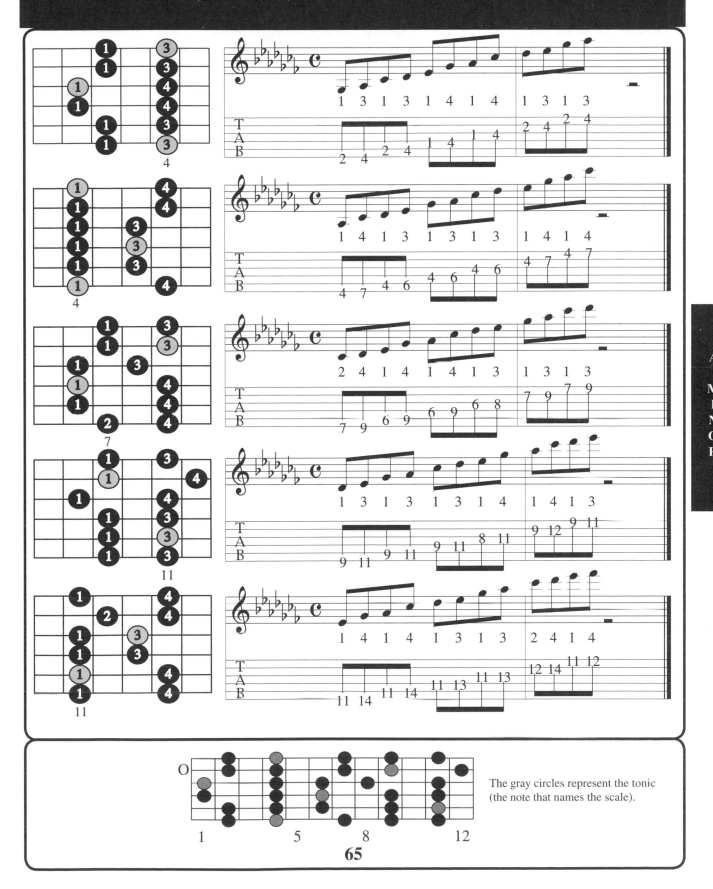

The gray circles represent the tonic (the note that names the scale).

THE DOMINANT PENTATONIC SCALES

Scale Degrees:	1	2	3	5	♭7	(1)
Intervals:		whole step	whole step	1 1/2 steps	1 1/2 steps	whole step
		C	D	E	G	B♭	C

Example:
C dominant
pentatonic

DOMINANT PENTATONIC SCALE PATTERNS

The gray circles represent the tonic (the note that names the scale).

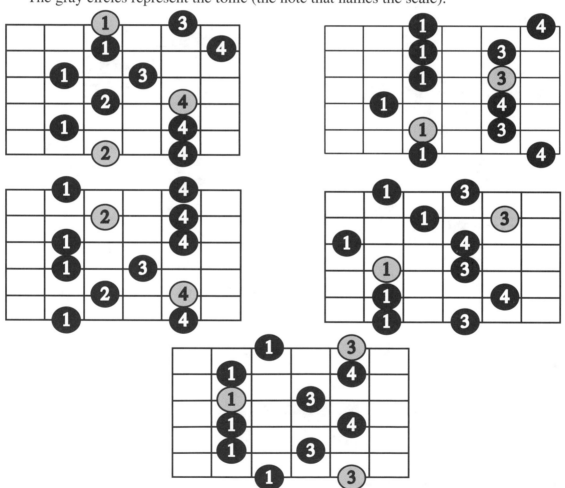

The dominant pentatonic scale is a five-note scale. It is a variation of the major pentatonic scale, replacing the sixth degree with a flat seven.

Suggestions for usage: Primarily used over dominant seventh chords. Also used over chord progressions containing the flat seven. May be used over any type of music.

Example: A dominant pentatonic scale over A7 or A to G chord progression. Try B♭ dominant pentatonic over track 10 of the *Let's Jam! CD Jazz & Blues*. E dominant pentatonic sounds good over track 10 of the *Let's Jam! CD Blues & Rock*.

66

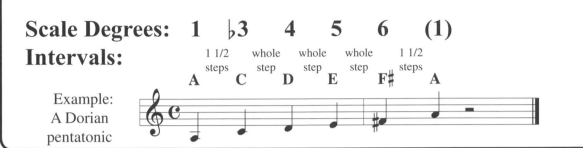

Scale Degrees: 1 ♭3 4 5 6 (1)

Intervals:

Example: A Dorian pentatonic

DORIAN PENTATONIC SCALE PATTERNS

The gray circles represent the tonic (the note that names the scale).

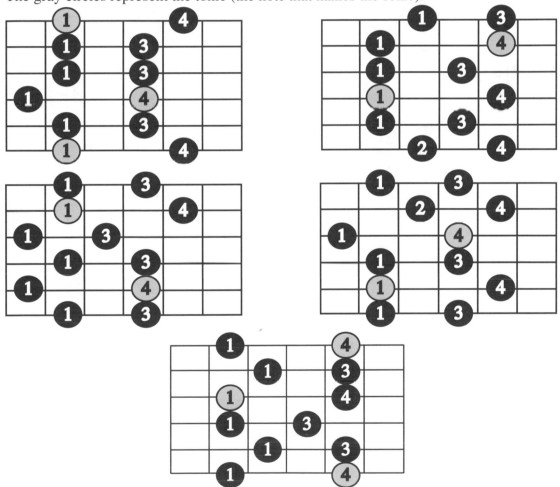

The Dorian pentatonic scale is a five-note scale. It is a variation of the minor pentatonic scale, replacing the seventh degree with a sharp six.

Suggestions for usage: Primarily used over minor seventh chords and tunes in a minor key with a Dorian sound. May be used over any type of music.

Example: A Dorian pentatonic scale over Am7 or Am6. Great over Am7-D9. Try B Dorian pentatonic over track 11 of *Let's Jam! CD Blues and Rock*.

DORIAN PENTATONIC

THE DORIAN MODE

Scale Degrees:	1	2	♭3	4	5	6	♭7	(1)
Intervals:		whole step	half step	whole step	whole step	whole step	half step	whole step

Example:
A Dorian

A B C D E F♯ G A

DORIAN SCALE PATTERNS

The gray circles represent the tonic (the note that names the scale).

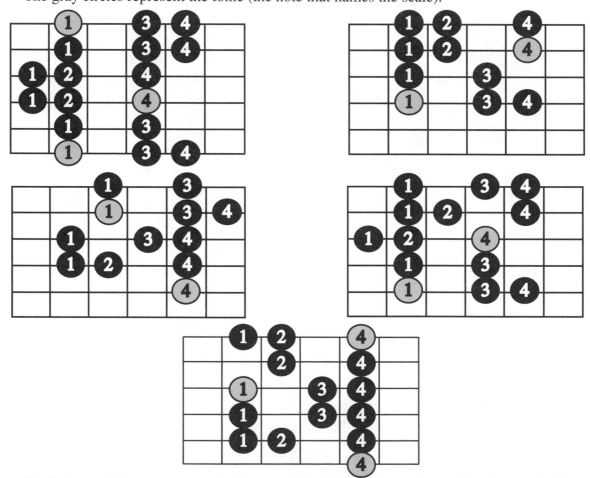

The Dorian mode is a seven-note scale. You may think of this scale several ways. Most importantly, it is a minor scale with a raised sixth degree. You may also play a major scale one whole step lower than the minor chord or the minor key you are in. This equals the Dorian mode. (Example: The G major scale =A Dorian) Another way to think of it is playing a major scale, starting and ending on the second degree.

Suggestions for usage: Primarily used over minor chords and over certain chord progressions including the raised sixth degree. Try this scale over jazz, blues, rock, etc.

Example: A Dorian mode over Am7 or A Dorian over Am7-D9 (D9 would contain the natural sixth degree, in this case, F♯). Try B Dorian over track 11 of the *Let's Jam CD! Blues and Rock*.

THE MIXOLYDIAN MODE

Scale Degrees:	1	2	3	4	5	6	♭7	(1)
Intervals:		whole step	whole step	half step	whole step	whole step	half step	whole step

Example:
C Mixolydian

C D E F G A B♭ C

MIXOLYDIAN SCALE PATTERNS

The gray circles represent the tonic (the note that names the scale).

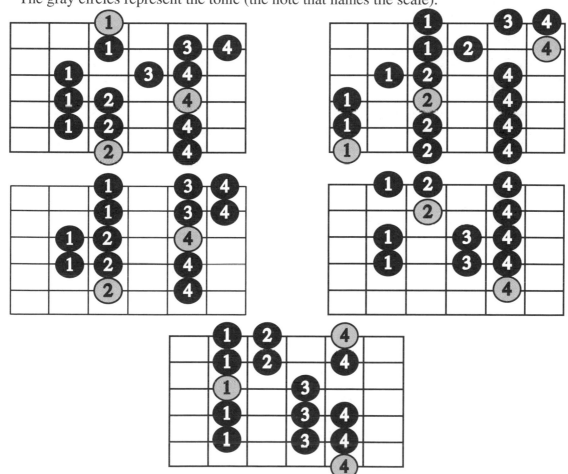

The Mixolydian mode is a seven-note scale. You may think of this scale several ways. Most importantly, it is a major scale with a flat seventh degree. You may also play a major scale a perfect fourth higher than the dominant seventh chord or major key you are in. This equals the Mixolydian mode. (Example: D Major =A Mixolydian) Another way to think of it is playing a major scale starting and ending on the fifth degree.

Suggestions for usage: Primarily used over dominant seventh chords and over certain chord progressions in a major key including the flatted seventh degree. Try this scale over jazz, blues, rock, etc.

Example: C Mixolydian mode over C7 or C Mixolydian over C-B♭ chord progression. Try B♭ Mixolydian over track 10 of the *Let's Jam! CD Jazz & Blues*.

69

Scale Degrees:	1	2	3	♯4	5	6	7	(1)
Intervals:		whole step	whole step	whole step	half step	whole step	whole step	half step

Example: C Lydian

C D E F♯ G A B C

LYDIAN SCALE PATTERNS

The gray circles represent the tonic (the note that names the scale).

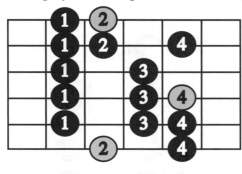

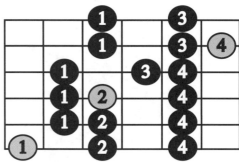

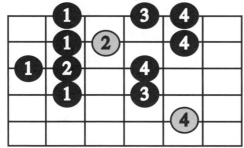

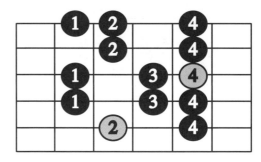

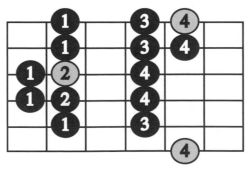

The Lydian mode is a seven-note scale. You may think of this scale several ways. Most importantly, it is a major scale with a raised fourth degree. You may also play a major scale a perfect fifth higher than the major chord or major key you are in. This equals the Lydian mode. Another way to think of it is playing a major scale starting and ending on the fourth degree.

Suggestions for usage: Primarily used over major chords and major sharp eleven chords. It is also interesting over a C power chord. Try this scale over jazz, blues, rock, etc.

Example: C Lydian mode over CM7 or C#11. Try E Lydian over track 11 of the *Let's Jam! CD Jazz & Blues*.

THE PHRYGIAN MODE

Scale Degrees:	1	♭2	♭3	4	5	♭6	♭7	(1)
Intervals:		half step	whole step	whole step	whole step	half step	whole step	whole step

Example:
A Phrygian

A   B♭   C   D   E   F   G   A

PHRYGIAN SCALE PATTERNS

The gray circles represent the tonic (the note that names the scale).

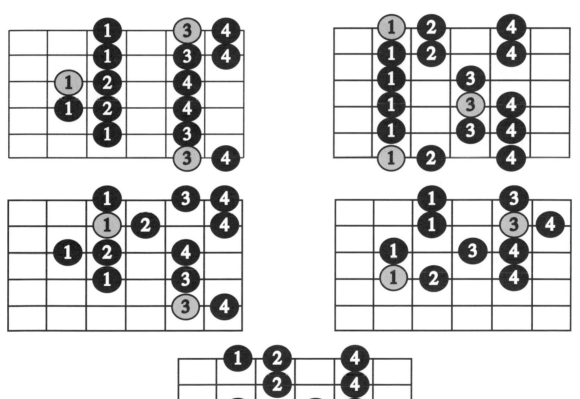

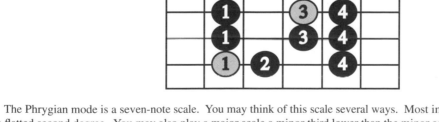

The Phrygian mode is a seven-note scale. You may think of this scale several ways. Most importantly it is a minor scale with a flatted second degree. You may also play a major scale a minor third lower than the minor seventh chord or minor key you are in. This equals the Phrygian mode. Another way to think of it is playing a major scale starting and ending on the third degree.

Suggestions for usage: Primarily used over minor chords. It is also interesting over a power chord. Try this scale over jazz, blues, rock, etc.

Example: A Phrygian mode over Am7.

71

THE LOCRIAN MODE

Scale Degrees:	1	♭2	♭3	4	♭5	♭6	♭7	(1)
Intervals:		half step	whole step	whole step	half step	whole step	whole step	whole step

Example:
A Locrian

A B♭ C D E♭ F G A

LOCRIAN SCALE PATTERNS

The gray circles represent the tonic (the note that names the scale).

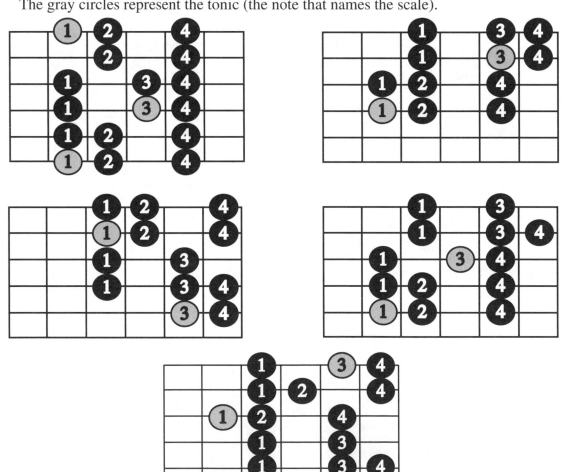

The Locrian mode is a seven-note scale. You may think of this scale several ways. Most importantly it is a minor scale with a flatted second and flatted fifth degree. You may also play a major scale a half step higher than the minor chord or minor key you are in. This equals the Locrian mode. Another way to think of it is playing a major scale starting and ending on the seventh degree.

Suggestions for usage: Primarily used over minor seven flat five or diminished seventh chords.

Example: A Locrian mode over Am7 flat 5 or A diminished 7th.

EXPLAINING THE MODES

When guitar players first hear the word *mode*, they think of some complicated concept that brings fear into their hearts. When I was first taught modes in college, I was taught the concept in a manner that was impractical and difficult to understand. Let's try to make it simple and useful.

First, whenever you hear the word mode, substitute the word scale, because that's what they really are: simply scales. We can get more analytical and justify the name mode, but let's just think scale.

WHY USE MODES?

A mode is a variation of a scale you probably already know. It's used to fit with the chord or chords you are playing over. For example, if you are playing over a G7 chord, the G major scale will conflict with one of the notes in the chord. The seventh in the G major scale is F sharp, where the seventh in the G7 chord is F natural. Instead of using G major, use G Mixolydian, which contains all the notes of the G major scale, but with a F natural instead of a F sharp.

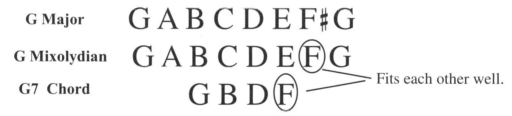

G Major	G A B C D E F♯ G
G Mixolydian	G A B C D E Ⓕ G
G7 Chord	G B D Ⓕ — Fits each other well.

Here's the reason for using modes. ***We use modes to fit over the chord or chords we are playing***. Let's examine all our modes and learn when to use them.

THE DORIAN MODE

The Dorian mode is generally used over minor chords and certain minor chord progressions. I think of the Dorian mode as a variation of the minor scale. Here is the A minor scale.

A B C D E F G A

The Dorian mode is the same scale, but with a raised sixth degree (F sharp). Here is the A Dorian mode.

A B C D E F♯ G A

We can use the Dorian mode over any minor chord, but I like to look at the chord progression to indicate whether to use A minor or A Dorian. If I am playing the chord progression Am7-Dm7, I'll likely use the A minor scale. If I am playing Am7 to D9, I'll likely use A Dorian because the chord D9 has a F sharp in it. The F sharp indicates A Dorian.

Dm7   **D F A C**

D9   **D F♯ A C E**

When deciding between using a minor scale or a Dorian mode, look at the notes in the chord and the chord progression. If it is a static chord progression, a long time spent on just the minor chord, you may use either.

LOCATING THE DORIAN MODE

Here is a trick for finding the Dorian mode quickly. If you examine the A Dorian scale and the G major scale, you'll find they have exactly the same notes.

A Dorian   **A B C D E F♯ G A**

G Major   **G A B C D E F♯ A**

This means G major equals A Dorian. ***To locate the Dorian mode of the chord you are playing over, simply go down a whole step from the root. Play a major scale starting on that note and you will be playing the Dorian mode.*** You may think of the Dorian mode in either of these two ways: a natural minor scale with a raised sixth degree or a major scale down one whole step from the minor chord or *key center* (the chord the music returns to) you are in.

We will not go into as much detail with the other modes, as they all will work under the same concept. For each mode, there will be a major scale with the same notes. For each mode, there are certain chords they are generally used over. Let's look at the rest of the modes.

THE MIXOLYDIAN MODE

The Mixolydian mode is generally used over dominant seventh chords or major chord progressions with a flat seven. Think of the Mixolydian mode as a major scale with a flat seven.

C D E F G A B C   C Major

C D E F G A B♭ C   C Mixolydian

C E G B♭   C7 chord

LOCATING THE MIXOLYDIAN MODE

To locate the Mixolydian mode, simply play a major scale a fourth higher than the chord or key center you are playing over. For example, the F major scale is the same as C Mixolydian.

C Mixolydian   C D E F G A B♭ C

F Major   F G A B♭ C D E F

This means F major equals C Mixolydian. You may think of the Mixolydian scale in either of two ways: a major scale with a flat seventh degree or a major scale a fourth higher than the key center or chord you are playing over.

THE LYDIAN MODE

The Lydian mode is generally used over major chords and especially major chords with a sharp eleven. Think of the Lydian mode as a major scale with a raised fourth degree. Let's compare the C major scale and the C Lydian mode.

C Major   C D E F G A B C

C Lydian   C D E F♯ G A B C

C Major chord   C E G

C#11 chord   C E G D F♯

LOCATING THE LYDIAN MODE

To locate the Lydian mode, simply play a major scale a fifth higher than the chord or key you are playing over. For example, the G major scale is the same as C Lydian.

C Lydian   C D E F♯ G A B C

G Major   G A B C D E F♯ G

This means G major equals C Lydian. You may think of the Lydian mode in either of two ways: a major scale with a raised fourth or a major scale starting a fifth higher than the chord or major key center you are playing over.

THE PHRYGIAN MODE

The Phrygian mode is generally used over minor chords. Think of the Phrygian mode as a minor scale with a flatted second degree. Let's compare A natural minor with A Phrygian.

A Minor	A B C D E F G A
A Phrygian	A B♭ C D E F G A
A Minor chord	A C E

LOCATING THE PHRYGIAN MODE

To find the Phrygian mode, simply play a major scale a major third lower than the chord or key center you are playing over. For example, F major is the same as A Phrygian.

| A Phrygian | A B♭ C D E F G A |
| F Major | F G A B♭ C D E F |

This means F major equals A Phrygian. You may think of the Phrygian mode in either of two ways: the natural minor scale with a flatted second degree or the major scale starting a major third lower than the chord or key center you are playing over.

THE LOCRIAN MODE

The Locrian mode is generally used over minor chords, especially minor seven flat five chords and diminished chords. Think of the Locrian mode as a natural minor scale with a flatted second and fifth degree. Let's compare A natural minor with A Locrian.

A Minor	A B C D E F G A
A Locrian	A B♭ C D E♭ F G A
A Minor chord	A C E
A Minor 7 flat 5 chord	A C E♭ G
A Diminished chord	A C E♭

LOCATING THE LOCRIAN MODE

To locate the Locrian mode, simply play a major scale a half step higher than the chord or key center you are playing over. For example, lets compare A Locrian with B flat major

A Locrian A B♭ C D E♭ F G A

B flat Major B♭ C D E♭ F G A B

This means B flat major equals A Locrian. You may think of Locrian in either of 2 ways - a minor scale with a flatted second and flatted fifth or a major scale a half step higher than the chord or key center that your are in.

ONE LAST THOUGHT ABOUT MODES

You may realize now why the major scale is called the mother of all scales. When you know your major scales, you actually know all your modes as well. For example, when you play C major, you are also playing

A Minor, G Mixolydian, D Dorian, F Lydian, E Phrygian, B Locrian

All these scales have the same notes in them as C major and you can use the same fingerings, just a different tonic or root. A word of caution: understand that whatever key or chord you are playing over will change what notes are important in each scale. It is also very valuable to know each mode starting on it's tonic. In other words, playing A minor starting on A, G Mixolydian starting on G, D Dorian starting on D, etc. I also like to associate my modes with particular chords, so I can find them readily.

THE IONIAN AND AEOLIAN MODES

The Ionian mode is another name for the major scale and the Aeolian mode is another name for the minor scale. Since we have already discussed these scales previously in the book there is no need to explain them here.

Scale Degrees: 1 ♭3 4 ♭5 5 ♭7 (1)

Intervals: 1 1/2 steps whole step half step half step 1 1/2 steps whole step

Example: A blues

A C D E♭ E G A

BLUES SCALE PATTERNS

The gray circles represent the tonic (the note that names the scale).

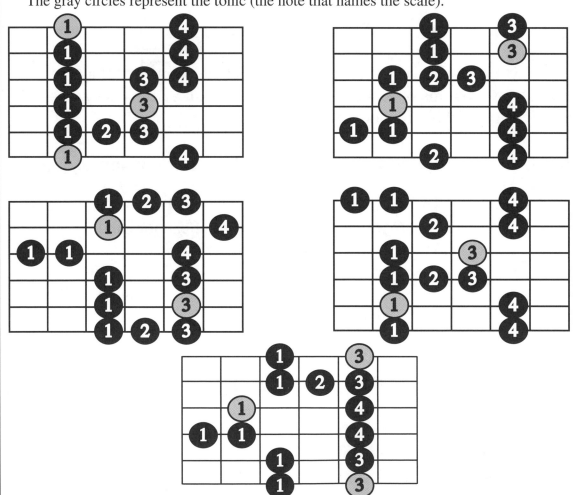

The blues scale is a six-note scale. It is very similar to the minor pentatonic scale, just add the flat five. Anytime you can use the minor pentatonic scale, you can also use the blues scale.

Suggestions for usage: Used in every genre of music. First, try it over minor chords or a song in a minor key. Then try it over blues, rock, jazz, etc.

Example: A blues scale over Am7 chord or the 12 bar blues in A minor or A major. The A blues scale sounds great over track 4 of the *Let's Jam! CD Blues & Rock*.

THE WHOLE TONE SCALES

Scale Degrees:	1	2	3	♭5	♭6	♭7	(1)
Intervals:		whole step	whole step	whole step	whole step	whole step	whole step

Example:
A whole tone

A   B   C♯   E♭   F   G   A

WHOLE TONE SCALE PATTERNS

The gray circles represent the tonic (the note that names the scale).

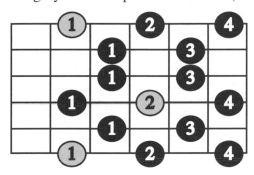

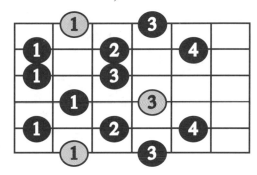

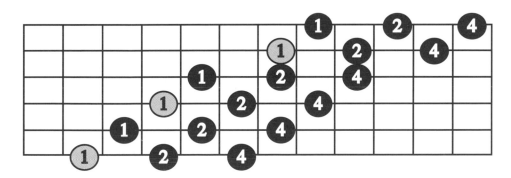

The whole tone scale is considered a symmetrical scale because it repeats itself every two frets. Simply learn the scale, then play it starting two frets higher or lower, and you are playing the same set of notes.

Suggestions for usage: Primarily used in jazz. Try it over a dominant seventh or play it a half step higher over a dominant seventh chord. In the latter case, be sure to resolve to a chord tone.

Example: A whole tone scale over A7, A7#5, or A augmented. Try E whole tone over track 4 of the *Let's Jam! CD Blues & Rock*.

THE DIMINISHED SCALES

Scale Degrees:	1	2	♭3	4	♭5	♭6	6	7	(1)
Intervals:		whole step	half step	whole step	half step	whole step	half step	whole step	half step
Example: A diminished	A	B	C	D	E♭	F	F♯	G♯	A

DIMINISHED SCALE PATTERNS

The gray circles represent the tonic (the note that names the scale).

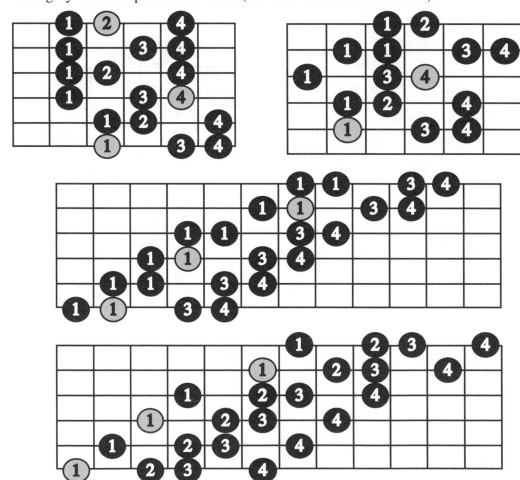

The diminished scale is considered a symmetrical scale because it repeats itself every three frets or every minor third. Simply learn the scale, then play it starting three frets higher and you are playing the same set of notes.

Suggestions for usage: Primarily used in jazz. Try it over a diminished chord or a minor 7th. Try playing it a half step higher over a dominant 7th chord, just be sure to resolve to a chord tone.

Example: A diminished scale over Adim7 or Am7. Bb diminished over A7 with a flat 9.

80

Scale Degrees:	1	♭2	♭3	♭4	♭5	♭6	♭7	(1)
Intervals:		half step	whole step	half step	whole step	whole step	whole step	whole step
Example: A altered dominant	A	B♭	C	D♭	E♭	F	G	A

ALTERED DOMINANT SCALE PATTERNS

The gray circles represent the tonic (the note that names the scale).

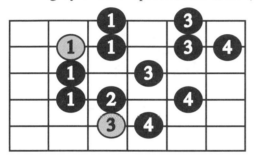
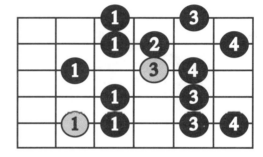
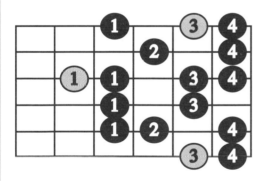
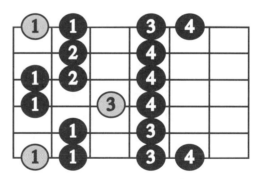

The altered dominant scale is a seven-note scale. It is actually a mode of the melodic minor scale. It is the same as playing the melodic minor scale starting on the seventh degree and ending on the seventh degree. It is called the altered dominant scale because it contains the notes which makes an altered dominant chord. The sharp or flat nine and the sharp or flat five.

Suggestions for usage: Primarily used in jazz. It is generally used over the five chord. It's job is to create tension that is resolved or released when the one chord arrives.

Example: A altered dominant scale over A7alt or just plain A7, resolving on a D chord. Try this over the five chord on any track of the *Let's Jam! CD Jazz & Blues*.

Scale Degrees:	1	2	3	4	5	6	♭7	7	(1)
Intervals:		whole step	whole step	half step	whole step	whole step	half step	half step	half step

BEBOP SCALES AND LINES

The gray circles represent the tonic (the note that names the scale).

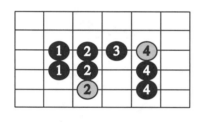

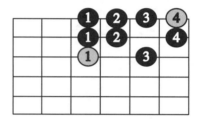

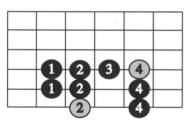

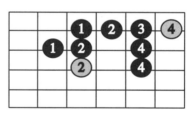

The bebop scales are more a method of playing than a set of scales. Think of them as a variation of the mixolydian scale only with an extra note, the sharp seventh. This note was added to make the line, or scale, smoother when played in rhythm. The major and mixolydian scales end oddly on the last eighth note of the measure when played in constant eighth notes.

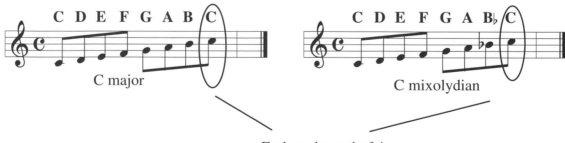

End on the and of 4.

The bebop scale, however, ends on a strong downbeat.

C bebop

The theory is that this leads to smoother lines when improvising. Bebop is a chromatic, smooth sound and is more an approach to improvising than a scale. Listening to bebop and imitating the sound of bebop is the best way to understand it. There are some stock licks and endings used when playing bebop. Here are a few of them:

Bebop Ending 1

Bebop Ending 2

Bebop Ending 3

Bebop Lick 1

Bebop Lick 2

When using bebop over minor chords, you may use the same lines and scales as when playing over a dominant seventh chord. Simply take the bebop scale you know and apply it over a minor chord, a fifth higher. For example, bebop over Gm7 would be the same scale used for playing over C7 (G is a fifth higher than C).

83

Hungarian Major

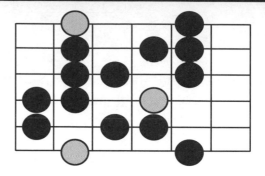

Hungarian Minor

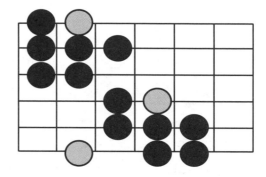

Hungarian Gypsy

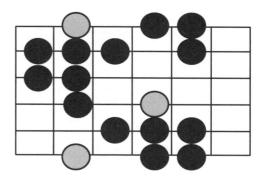

Iwato (Japan)

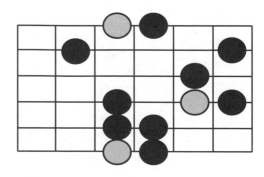

The gray circles represent the tonic (the note that names the scale).

Neopolitan Major

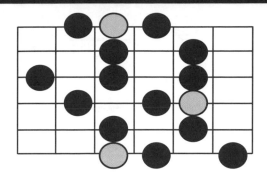

Neopolitan Minor

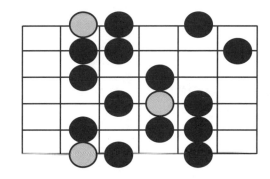

Persian

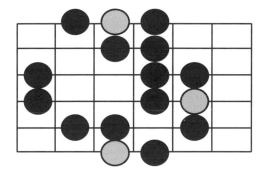

Spanish

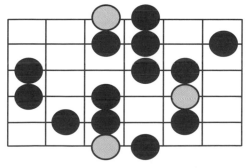

The gray circles represent the tonic (the note that names the scale).

FIRST POSITION DIATONIC SCALES

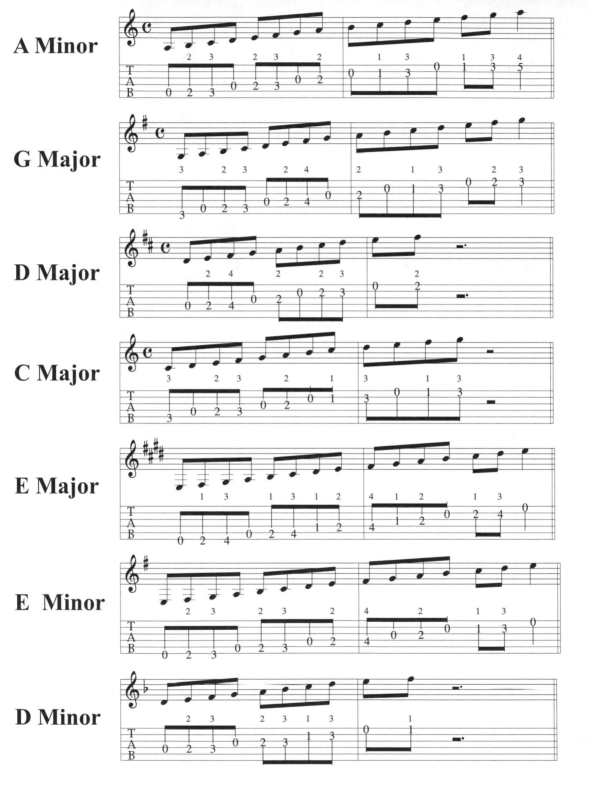

You may wish to try alternate fingerings for speed and fluidity. Try 1 and 3 in place of 2 and 4 and 1 and 2 in place of 2 and 3.

CROSS STRINGING SCALES

Cross stringing scales are scales that spread out the notes across strings rather than playing them from one string to the next in a logical fashion. Incorporating open strings gives these scales a cascading *legato* sound. Not all scales work well with this technique. Sharp keys or scales that use notes played on open strings work best. Here are some examples. On this page are straight major scales. On the next are chromatic cross stringing scales that go in and out of the scale.

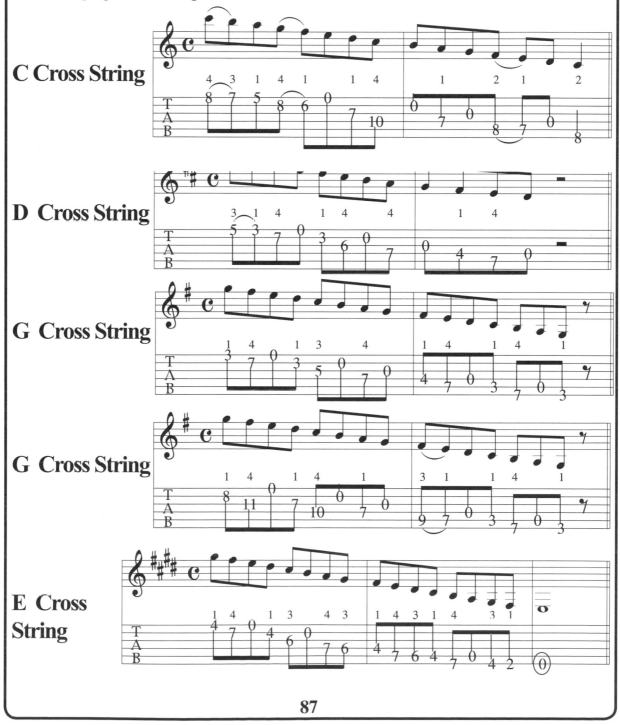

C Cross String

D Cross String

G Cross String

G Cross String

E Cross String

87

CROSS STRINGING SCALES

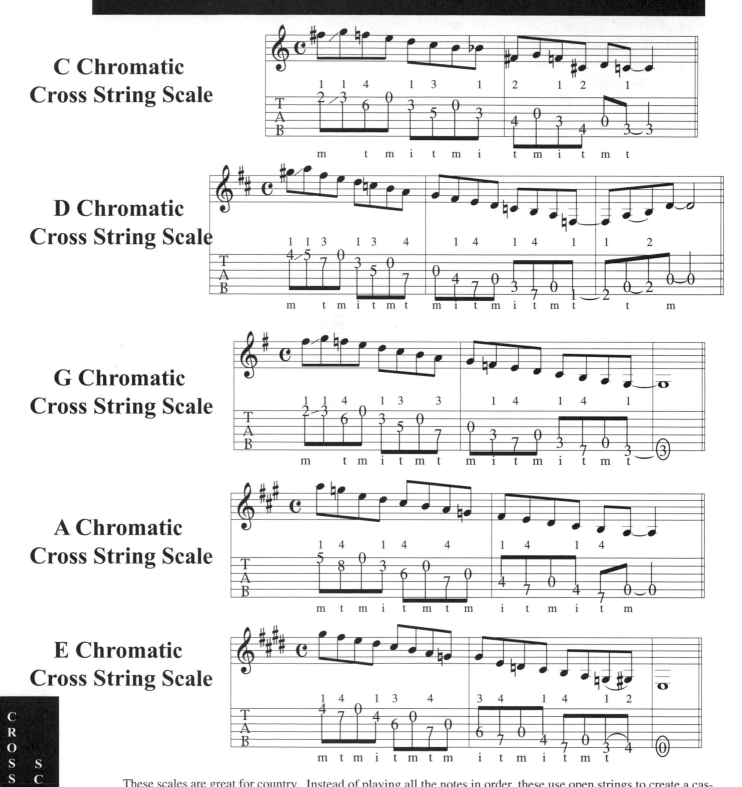

C Chromatic Cross String Scale

D Chromatic Cross String Scale

G Chromatic Cross String Scale

A Chromatic Cross String Scale

E Chromatic Cross String Scale

These scales are great for country. Instead of playing all the notes in order, these use open strings to create a cascade like effect.